Sky Hig..

MW00656909

No Goal Is Out of Your Reach

By Dr. Irene Trowell-Harris

Adducent

VETERANS PUBLISHING SYSTEMS
Writing & Publishing Assistance for Veterans

Jacksonville, Florida—Herndon, Virginia
www.AdducentInc.com

Sky High

No Goal Is Out of Your Reach

By Dr. Irene Trowell-Harris
as told to Dennis M. Lowery

ISBN 978-0-9777884-2-2

Library of Congress Control Number: 2009942914

Published by Adducent, Inc. – Veterans Publishing Systems

Jacksonville, Florida—Herndon, Virginia

www.AdducentInc.com

Manufactured in the United States of America

In Memory

This book is dedicated to the memory of my mother Irene Battle Trowell, the family icon, brothers Dr. Jack Trowell, a brilliant physician and mentor and Lee Trowell, my best friend and confidant. They all deserve awards and recognition for their contributions to country, state, community and family.

Dedication

This book is also dedicated to my remaining brothers and sisters: Frances Gomillion, Mae Brown, Sherry Diane Perry, Lafayette, Franklin and Crey Trowell. To the past, present and future students that I have mentored and will mentor—thank you for rewarding experiences past and those yet to come.

As children, we wished that we could reach up into the sky, and touch a star...

Sometimes a star reaches out, and touches us.

It is hereby declared to be the policy of the President that there shall be equality of treatment and opportunity for all persons in the armed services without regard to race, color, religion or national origin.

- President Harry S. Truman, Executive Order 9981: July 26, 1948. E. David Cronon, "Twentieth Century America, Vol. 2" (1996 page 449).

"It seemed like a long way from 143rd street. Shaking hands with the Queen of England was a long way from being forced to sit in the colored section of the bus going into downtown Wilmington, North Carolina."

- Althea Gibson (after winning the women's singles title at Wimbledon, 1957). "Women-Sports Magazine", March 1976.

"White nurses were called 'Miss'—black nurses were just 'nurse'."

- Dr. Irene Trowell-Harris (recounting the beginning of her nursing career in 1956)

"If I am right, the problem that has no name stirring in the minds of so many American women today is not a matter of loss of femininity or too much education, or the demands of domesticity. It is far more important than anyone recognizes. It is the key to these other old and new problems which have been torturing women and their husbands and children and puzzling their doctors and educators for years. It may well be the key to our future as a nation and a culture. We can no longer ignore that voice within women that says: "I want something more than my husband and my children and my home."

- Betty Friedan, "The Feminine Mystique" (1963 page 27).

"You can never have a greater or less dominion than over yourself."

- Leonardo da Vinci

"The average person puts only 25% of their energy and ability into their work. The world takes off its hat to those who put in more than 50% of their capacity, and stands on its head for those few and far between souls who devote 100%."

- Andrew Carnegie

"Your whole life comes alive when you have the determination to follow a dream, to create change, to do what is right over what is easy, and the courage to value tomorrow as much as you do today."

- Dr. Irene Trowell-Harris

Contents

Acknowledgements

As with any work of this magnitude, this book is the result of the efforts and collaboration of numerous people, both civilian and military.

So many individuals educated me, mentored me and offered me challenging opportunities to excel over the span of my life. At the risk of attempting to list all individuals, I will list some and other names may be omitted, however their assistance was and is just as important.

After considering for many years, that I should write a book and collecting information on and reviewing various publishing companies and ghostwriter services to help me, I decided in August 2009 that it was "now or never".

Interestingly, about that same time, I read an e-mail message from a flag officer website about a company interested in working with general officers to help them write and publish books. After sending an e-mail message to them asking for more information, I immediately received an e-mail back with some information and a draft book-cover image. That is when I first met Dennis Lowery, a super star!

I would like to start by thanking my key mentor Major General Paul Weaver, Jr., USAF (Retired) for his confidence in me and for taking the risk of appointing me as commander of the 105 USAF Clinic, Newburgh, New York. It was something never done before and I know he took flak for it but I think I proved him right! There is a close link between his confidence in me and my career progression and perseverance in writing this book.

I also want to thank Lieutenant General John Conway, USAF (Retired) and Lieutenant General Russell Davis, USAF (Retired) – both were crucial to my progress to general officer rank.

Special appreciation goes to my early mentors and military colleagues throughout my career: Major General Charles Cooper, III, USAF (Retired); Brigadier General Sharon Mailey, USAF (Retired); Brigadier General Sue Turner, USAF (Retired); Brigadier General Wilma Vaught, USAF (Retired);

Brigadier General Sarah Wells, USAF (Retired); Brigadier General Barbara Goodwin, USAF (Retired); Brigadier General Linda Stierle, USAF (Retired); Colonel Patricia Porter, USAF (Retired); Dr. (Colonel) Andrew Buzzelli, USAF (Retired); Lieutenant Colonel Beatrice Goodwin, USAF (Retired); Lieutenant Colonel Glen Fraser, NYANG; Chief Ed Ladson, USAF (Retired), and TSGT Mary Pilgrim, USAF (Retired).

I also wish to thank my professors at Jersey City State University, Yale and Columbia for their mentoring and guidance in support of my advanced education.

Special thanks to my colleagues at the Aiken County Historical Museum: Elliott Levy, Director, Mary White and Brenda Baratto, VA staff members and colleagues of Mt. Olive Baptist Church.

I give praise to my brothers and sisters whom supported me over the years and attended my promotions and retirement ceremonies in Washington. They all added value to my life in uniquely different ways. Special recognition to Lafayette Trowell and Inez Trowell who helped take care of our mother by relocating her in their home the last 18 months of her life.

High praise for uncle, Reverend Jacob C. Trowell who was always there for the family offering support, advice and spiritual guidance.

Finally, I could not have written this book without the advice and support of Dennis M. Lowery, President of Adducent, Inc. I was consistently amazed by his advice, creativity, and ability to describe situations with clarity and simplicity. I have great respect and admiration for him, his editors and the supporting staff, led by his oldest daughter Karen Lowery at Adducent and their publishing imprints.

Introduction

"Life is one-tenth here and now, nine-tenths a history lesson."

- Graham Swift, "Waterland" (1983 chapter 8).

"Since my release I have become more convinced than ever that the real makers of history are the ordinary men and women of our country; their participation in every decision about the future is the only guarantee of true democracy and freedom."

- Nelson Mandela, "The Struggle of My Life" (1990)

Since graduating high school in 1956, I've lived a sheaf of years.

In that time, like many, I've enjoyed the good that life brings, and endured—in some cases—overcame the bad.

I hope and believe that I, and my generation, faced challenges, which younger generations did not or will not encounter. And in our facing them, perhaps helped bring about the positive changes that makes this world today, better in some respects than it was then, and more importantly sets a direction for even further improvements.

Nine-tenths of my life's experience embodied a belief in self-determination and its daily application. I hope the readers of this book, draw strength from that and use that same belief to prevail against the challenges they face in their own life—positively affecting the "nine-tenths" of their own lives that they will reflect on years from now. And that one day they find in their own fashion, as ordinary men and women—they too influenced their own and other people's futures in a good way.

This book is different from the usual memoir.

It is not meant to be a "see what I've done" type of book. It is a chronicling of personal achievements and key accomplishments as you would see in a normal memoir, but written as an inspirational tool to inspire others for success.

 As you read, the symbol you see to the left will signify important tips or lessons I've learned that might be of help to you. Highlight the ones that you feel are most meaningful to you.

I believe in self-determination. Take ownership in your life; in all that you do, whether you are at the top of your profession, just starting out or at any other level in between those two points—do the very best job that you can do. Do this wherever you may be and whatever position you may find yourself in.

Where you are, is where you are starting from—don't think a "better time" will come—don't expect that someone is going to hand you the solution or an easy way to make a great leap forward.

You have to find it within yourself to create your own destiny. No matter what has happened or not happened in the past—take your future in hand and shape the one that you want.

This book is an overview of an entire life, highlighting milestones and certain significant periods, points of decision and turning points in my life. Some of which are similar to those that many people encounter. Perhaps hearing of my decisions and thought process leading to them will help you with yours.

The first purpose of this book is to demonstrate that anyone with even the humblest beginnings can become successful beyond their wildest imagination.

My journey started in a cotton field in Aiken, South Carolina and has taken me to dozens of countries, a 38-year military career where I rose to become a Major General (2-stars) and became a White House political appointee.

Very far indeed for a young black girl who while picking cotton in the mid-1950s, looked up at a plane in the sky and dreamed of flying.

The second purpose of this book is to serve as an inspirational tool for youth and those adults stuck-in-place needing a little encouragement to jump-start their careers. Rarely is there anything "new under the sun" when it comes to the problems and challenges that people are faced with in life.

It is not what you are faced with that is the important issue of your life. It is how you respond. It is how you deal with things.

I believe that in today's very busy world with almost "push-button" gratification for any thing we need and the "instant" answer capability of the internet we forget that often the answers, to the truly important questions we have, lay within ourselves.

Never forget that ultimately, deep inside yourself is where you need to find strength and determination to make changes in your life, to deal with problems and issues that you face—and to learn from them so that you can share a positive lesson and improve the lives of those around you.

Learning from others who have faced and solved significant problems and overcome serious obstacles can help you find that seed of strength within yourself. Open your eyes and ears to that world of experience—let it help you.

On that note, many people have inspired, educated, and mentored me throughout my life and successful military and civilian careers. In the telling, of my story perhaps you will recognize something familiar in them, and in your own life maybe a person or someone you know—becomes the mentor or inspiration that can help you, in the same way as mine have helped me.

With most stories, the question is where to start and how to make it a compelling heartwarming story, appealing, inspirational, eye-catching (and eye-holding) and dynamic. In fiction, they tell the writer to put the reader immediately into the scene, with the protagonist in jeopardy, thereby hooking the reader immediately, making them interested to see what happens next. My life has been an adventure but not necessarily an "adventure story" ... but let me tell you about how it was for me ... in my beginning.

Chapter One ~ The Beginning

"The Cotton Fields"

I seemed on fire; the sand burning my feet, a searing heat that never let up—making you want to step faster just for the flash of relief when your foot left the smoldering ground. The heat like a wine press on my head squeezing a flow of stinging sweat into my eyes. Wiping them constantly, a sweep of my hand or sopping kerchief only gave a moment's pause ... then stinging again as the unending stream poured into my eyes. Drops of it fall like rain with each stoop and bend. I could feel it pool in my ears, spilling from them like small pitchers as my head turned and moved with the work. My shoulders and neck caught every pounding ray of sun, the only break as a cloud comes over, a small blessing, a shield from the beating of the sun—a breeze, the promise (sometimes false) of relief from the stifling heat that wraps a cotton field with you inside it.

Stoop labor—I knew the definition of it before I ever knew there was such a word. Bend, pick, pull and strip—put the cotton in my bag—do it all again. Over and over, hundreds of times in the heat—thousands of times throughout a full week of work. Fighting the lizards, insects, boll weevils and snakes that infest a cotton field. They wanted to be there—I sure didn't but had no choice.

Eyes stinging, hands and forearms scratched and cut—always roughed up—never healing. The ache in your back, shoulders and how your thigh muscles would feel after only a short while in the field. The chafing under the arms as my shirt, soaked even early in the day, rubbed away skin as my body went through the mechanical motions that had not changed in a hundred years—maybe more. A never-ending cycle—the worst kind of backbreaking work there is. Monday through Friday and a half day on Saturday. It is what I and my ten brothers and sisters had to do, part of what you have to do when you're a family and it depends on each person's efforts. For my family and many like mine it was the past, the present and the future. A bleak and hard life that many never got ahead of or away from.

One day when I was about 15, another day in the crucible—I straightened, stretching to relieve the strain on my back, blinking the sweat out of my eyes. I heard a sound, looked up and sun-sparked metal caught my eye. At first I couldn't spot what caused it, but seeing and following the long white line in the sky, at its end and highest point I saw the plane, a tiny cross of silver ... moving higher and farther away from me while I watched it. Sweat no longer gathering in my eyes, running down the sides of my face—I could see clearly now—clear and crisp, sharp like the stars on a winter night. In that moment, the line in the sky, drawn by the small cross of metal that moved with such purpose, I knew what I wanted to do—I knew I would find a way to leave the cotton fields behind me. I'd reach for and take in my hand, something that when I talked about it even amongst family made them smile and laugh—to fly and work on airplanes. To travel in the cool sky on silver wings—leaving a line just like the one above me, marking where I'd been and proof that I was going somewhere.

"Girl, how you going to do it?" they asked. They all knew a girl from a poor black family, farmers with little education and no money did not have a chance. Not in 1950s South Carolina. But I knew I could and some day, in some way ... I would ... leave that cotton field behind me and never return to it or another.

* * *

I was born in Aiken, South Carolina on September 20, 1939, the third of eleven children (three sisters and seven brothers) to Irene Battle Trowell and Frank Trowell.

We grew up and worked on a small cotton farm. During that time in the South, Black families worked on the farm and children only attended school once the crops were completely harvested. Early on, we used a mule and wagon for transportation since we did not own a car.

On the farm, we raised chickens, pigs, cows, turkeys, cotton, corn, peas, watermelons and assorted vegetables in the garden. We boiled our clothes in a pot with homemade lye soap (trust me you never want to get that in your eyes). We bathed in a tin tub with well water and had an outhouse for a bathroom.

As a family, we attended church most of the day on Sundays, first for Sunday school then the regular Baptist church service that lasted the rest of the day on occasions.

As a family, we also ate together for breakfast and supper every day. There was a prayer of thanks before each meal. On Sunday morning, we had a special breakfast of homemade rolls, grits, bacon, and cheese with eggs. That was a wonderful family treat.

My father and mother both had only a third grade education but were wise in what they wanted for their children. My parents taught me and my brothers and sisters, strong family values, a commitment to excellence in work ethic and a good religious foundation. They taught us discipline and helped us structure our lives and careers. Our mother especially, consistently stressed the value of getting a good education. *The things they taught me have been the bedrock of every success in my life.* As the children reached 10th grade in high school, in addition to farm work, we got jobs in local fast food restaurants to supplement the family income.

My mother's name "Irene Battle Trowell" held within it something that was more than just the name that she passed on to me. Something appropriate about how she approached life and an important lesson and philosophy she bestowed on her children. "Battle" in its finest sense means to strive, keep trying—don't quit. It's an indomitable spirit that gives the strength and will to face challenges in life head on and through determination, overcome them.

My mother always told us *"stay in school and stay in church, and you'll be fine."* Simple words, simple wisdom—yet powerful. She and my father raised eleven children of their own and seventeen foster-children. Following those words enabled many of them to have successful careers in medicine, aviation, nursing, law enforcement, small business and the military. I'm a perfect example of how following my mother's advice led to a career of accomplishment that I never imagined as a child and young woman. For young people—following those simple words can help you too!

* * *

I attended a segregated one-room school, Oakwood Elementary (known as Cushman Academy) in Aiken from first to eighth grade. My teachers Mrs. Hazel J. Cadle and Mrs. Alberta Scott taught all eight grades for $90.00 a month. I graduated in May 1952 and attended Martha Schofield High School for grades nine through twelve graduating as an honor student June 1956. I was May Day Beauty Queen and served as Class President in 11th grade. Other activities I was involved in included photo club, canteen assistant, hall patrol, NHA club and class officer. In addition, I was voted as one of the best-dressed senior students for 1956.

I was born with an insatiable desire to learn and to look at life differently. That in and of itself, conflicted with what society expected of women, and especially of women of my race, at that time. Women were expected to marry the local boy and have ten children to work on the farm and in the garden. I thought about that and decided I wanted to attend college and travel prior to getting married and having a family (but never ten children!).

Sad to say, but not uncommon at the time, for the most part, I was not advised or encouraged to attend college by most of my teachers. Some teachers assumed if you were low income, if your parents were not professionals and if you were from a large family, that there was no opportunity for college. That type of thinking unfortunately ruled out encouraging students to find alternative ways to find money for college—it was as if your life was set in a concrete path that could not be deviated from.

I wanted something different than what other people thought was my lot in life. I found through planning and work to follow the plan, that you can accomplish much in life that others may think can't be accomplished.

Since I was an honor student, I consulted with my homeroom teacher and the principal about my plans for after high school. They took interest, but waited until I was admitted to nursing school and could present one semester of grades. After that, I was given an annual scholarship. Opportunities generally come to you once you've proved yourself.

I had great respect for my homeroom teacher, Mrs. Lelia A. Bradby, a graduate of Hampton Institute and Cornell University with majors in English and French. She was very intelligent and had traveled extensively around the world. At first, she had misgivings because she saw so many poor children who would never find it within themselves to break free of poverty's stranglehold. Once she saw how serious I was and that I was committed to do what was necessary—to study as hard and as much as a I could—to work towards a goal—she always made time to talk with me about my hopes, dreams and plans. She gave me good advice and continued to mentor me even through nursing school.

After completing high school, I visited at intervals and received an invitation to speak to the student body after graduating from nursing school. Even then I felt a responsibility to share with others what I had done with the hope that they would see that they could follow their dreams too—even if it takes many small steps to get there instead of one large jump.

LESSONS LEARNED

Taking a leadership role and being proactive teaches you things that are important to success.

Don't assume that where you are, is where you have to stay. If you want something better—work towards it. Small steps can lead to big accomplishments.

Learn what you need to learn—do what you need to do—to put the past behind you and move forward to your future.

There is nothing wrong with hard, honest work. It can build a foundation that can carry you as high as you want to go.

Sometimes you have to prove yourself before opportunities appear. Waiting for one to come to you does not get it done. Create opportunities for yourself.

Chapter Two ~ Nursing School

"$60 dollars and a dream"

I reviewed the professional opportunities that were available to minority women in 1956 before graduating from high school. There were not many, the choice being becoming a teacher, nurse or secretary.

In the south, nurses and teachers were always employed, which meant one usually did not have to worry about finding a job and that provided a very practical economic reason for choosing one of them as a profession. I decided to become a nurse, something my mother had desired for her self but was unable to attend school because what she earned from working went to help her parents' survive financially—nothing was left to go towards nursing school. My mother always dreamed of becoming a nurse and that it was a path to making more money for her family. Her dreams were realized when my sister Mae, and I became nurses.

My mother's desire to go to nursing school made an impact on me but I was also influenced by meeting a nurse in our family doctors' medical office. At family doctor visits, she would always talk with me and was interested in how I was doing in school—she really cared that I was doing well and wanted to know about my plans for after high school. She would talk to me about what she thought about being a nurse and gave me brochures for different nursing schools so I could learn more about that as something to consider for after graduation. She believed that I would do well as a nurse. Her steady voice of support and confidence meant a lot and gave me an even stronger sense of determination to prove she was right about me.

Aside from the practical and economic attractiveness of nursing, a most compelling reason was the desire to care for and help others—a trait instilled in me by my mother and father. I felt then, and still do now, that my desire to become a nurse was a "divine calling" to help others not just a means to further my own interests. Nurses often consider their profession as a "calling." Florence Nightingale, the founder of modern nursing, characterized her spiritual motivation to serve others as an "inward tug."

My brothers, sisters and I were raised with a belief that we all have a responsibility to help those in need and to contribute in any way that we could. One of my brothers was born with cerebral palsy, was blind and unable to speak and our family members cared for him for 29 years until his death in 1969. I saw first-hand the importance of being a caregiver and that having a trained nurse in the family would have helped early on and did help once I became one.

After completing high school in June 1956, my desire was to attend A&T University in North Carolina, a four-year nursing university, but I did not have the initial $1,000 needed for tuition. My church, Mount Hill Baptist and high school, Martha Schofield united to share their financial resources with me by providing a scholarship for nursing school. In August

1956, I was accepted to attend a three-year nursing program, at a segregated school, Columbia Hospital School of Nursing in Columbia, South Carolina. My church collected $60 in nickels, dimes and quarters for my initial tuition payment and I relocated from Aiken to Columbia, South Carolina 70 miles from home. That $60 built the bridge I needed to get from the cotton fields to nursing school.

My family had a special dinner together on the Sunday before I drove to Columbia. My mother placed a $50 bill under my plate and wished me well in nursing school. Fifty dollars was a lot of money back then and quite a lot for my family. That was the first time I had seen a bill that large.

My first year of nursing school was a cultural shock since that was my first experience away from home. However, I was ecstatic about being admitted to nursing school and having the opportunity to learn a practical and valuable skill and to use it to help other people.

At school, I was paired with a student from Athens, Georgia. Ours was a twin bed room with a shared bathroom. We enjoyed each other's company, studied together and went to school social activities. I immediately bonded with my 38 classmates, and was excited about their stories and family history.

We all enjoyed the hospital type food and even had a different menu selection each day. During my first year there was very little free time, since I was extremely busy getting oriented to a new city, studying, networking with classmates, and working on hospital wards taking care of patients. During that time, I was also seeking a local church to attend and worship. I received several recommendations of various churches, visited most to check out the services and eventually selected a church to attend which proved to become like an extended family to me.

* * *

A Black Nurse in 1950s & 60s America: "White nurses were called 'Miss'—black nurses were just 'nurse'"

In nursing school, I found that black nurses were addressed as "nurse" while the white nurses were addressed as "Miss." I could not understand this distinction since we were all nurses. Nursing school was very challenging in the South for African American students; there were many barriers to success, such as race, ethnic background, social economic status, family size and gender. There were two separate schools in the same Columbia complex, one for white and one for black students. All instructors were white except one teacher, described by some students as a "light skin" lady from Florida. There were also separate dormitories for students and separate hospitals for white and black patients. Black students were not permitted in the dormitories or the hospital designated for whites.

At nursing school I was president of my class the junior and senior years and the social director for planning recreational events and class celebrations for three years. It was in my nature to be proactive, to participate and be part of the leadership of my class. I felt by taking on responsibility that it improved my capabilities and helped my classmates.

Though internally it helped me, positive recognition from my teachers for stepping up in that way was never given. My classmates and I were covertly discouraged from showing too much leadership ability or skills. We were not expected to seek promotions and move up the career ladder, as were the white students—we were relegated to bottom rung and expected to go no higher. It was an unwritten and silent rule that everybody appeared to understand or at least to adhere to. At first I attempted to understand, but could not internalize what it really meant and why it existed.

Discouragement only inspired me to push harder and reach for the stars! Even early on in my life and career I always worked with what I had at that time and began from where I stood. Always, I wanted to be an outstanding nurse striving for excellence in practice and academically.

A significant event happened my senior year of nursing school that forever changed my perception of authority and responsibility. As class president in coordination with my classmates, and with authorization from my faculty advisor I was given permission to identify psychiatric nursing training courses for black student nurses to attend at other institutions. Black nurses were not offered this at my nursing school—so it was something that we had to take separately, after graduation. When I was able to identify, in writing, available courses from New York State facilities for all my classmates, the faculty member denied she gave me permission, reprimanded me for unauthorized activity and threatened to expel me from nursing school. As punishment I was immediately placed on duty 10:00 a.m. to 7:00 p.m. alternating with night duty, and had to attend required classes during the day—leaving me very little time for sleep. The message was that I was not expected to be successful by that faculty member.

"As change occurs, you may have people attempting to keep you from succeeding."

- Indigo Triplett Johnson, "Playing by the Unwritten Rules--Moving from the middle to the top" (2006 page xii).

From that day forward, I questioned authority when what they were saying or doing "just did not make sense" to me. But—and this is an important lesson to learn, *you cannot defy or deny authority without an intelligent response.* To fight back or stand up based or fueled purely on emotion—can and does lead to destroying or damaging careers. One thing I have learned over a long life of ambition and pursuit of things not easily attained by those faced with challenges similar to mine—*by making decisions without thinking, or speaking without thought or intelligence—you cannot be heard and will not achieve anything positive.*

The greatest remedy for anger is delay

- Seneca

That same year, some of my classmates, during an upper class party for black students, were accused of entering a white dormitory recreation room and harassing students. The black students had set up the food and program in the approved recreation room, but later discovered white students eating their food. The white students were asked to leave the room and not to take the food. The white students reported the encounter as a racial incident. As the social director for my class, I with several of my classmates were questioned FBI style for hours, taken from one room, left by a second room and not allowed to speak with other students. I was working night duty and did not witness the incident since I was sleeping during the day. I was cleared of the charges, but threatened with expulsion if I discussed the incident. The pervasiveness of segregation confronted the black nurses at every turn. There were 39 students in my initial class at nursing school, only 12 of us graduated in 1959.

Even with challenges I faced at nursing school, I was an honor student, class social director and class president my 2nd and 3rd year. My management and leadership skills were evident early on, but as mentioned previously these efforts were discouraged in black students. When people attempted to discourage me, this actually motivated me to work harder for success. My success was not just for me, but also for my country, state, community, church and family. Even then, I had an insatiable desire to inspire and motivate others to become successful.

Although there were constant threats of expulsion from nursing school, we had a good time and enjoyed taking care of our patients. During my junior year, I was assigned to the ground floor of the dormitory initially with a roommate who smoked like a fiend, then a single room in my senior year with my own bathroom. This was heavenly and the first time in my life that I had my own room!

Just the freedom to go and do things with my friends was glorious. I had a classmate from Miami, Florida, Mary Adderley who owned an old car, which had a hole in the floorboard. You could see the street below as we drove around town, and when it rained its roof did not offer much protection. But it got us around! Since we were honor students, we could be out until 10:00 p.m. during the week. We went to movies, dances and fast food restaurants. Of course, we frequently checked out the handsome guys.

Like many young students, I tested the system. The housemother (called matrons) made rounds at 10:00 p.m. every night to make sure that we were in bed with the lights out. I made friends with several hospital kitchen employees and I frequently climbed out of my room window on the ground floor to get food from the hospital kitchen for my classmates. I would place a pillow covered with a blanket in my bed in case the housemother made rounds a second time, which she did occasionally to catch us disobeying the rules. Fortunately, I was never caught and enjoyed my small success at breaking the rules, but I definitely would not encourage this behavior in college students!

While at nursing school, I met Juanita and Andrew Martin whom became my adopted parents in Columbia, South Carolina. Juanita was a licensed practical nurse on the medical-surgical unit at

Columbia Hospital and Andrew a Mail Carrier. They entertained students with a warm family environment, unconditional love, great home cooked meals, barbecues, television and birthday parties. When we felt overwhelmed by the academic rigor of nursing school and being away from home, they comforted us just like our parents. Juanita and Andrew Martin celebrated their fiftieth wedding anniversary on June 2, 2001, which I attended with other Columbia Hospital graduates. I gave them a Waterford Crystal United States Capitol Dome and a plaque making them honorary parents for their unconditional love, inspiration and mentoring. We have kept in touch since 1956—still close even after 53 years.

I completed nursing school and graduated on Friday, September 5, 1959. I went to work at Talmadge Hospital in Augusta, Georgia on Monday, September 7, 1959, making $300.00 per month.

It has been 50 years since earning my nursing diploma (in September 1959) from Columbia Hospital School of Nursing (now the University of South

Carolina). Over that span I've also earned a bachelors degree from New Jersey City University, my masters degree from Yale and a doctorate from Columbia University; I have no doubt about my decision to become a nurse—and that continuing my education was the key to my success in life.

When I graduated from nursing school, I had a good-paying job (for that time) instead of rushing to buy a new car, new clothes, and a stereo; I invested in the human potential stock market of my family and myself. I feel strongly that the money you put into your own continuing education or to help family is more important than putting money into a shiny sports car, expensive clothes and things that you may not really need and that certainly will not give you a return on your "investment."

There was an urgent need for money for my parents and siblings since a storm in July destroyed major farm corps, such as cotton and corn the main source of family income for the year. These crops of cotton, corn and assorted vegetables were used to pay the annual farm bills and expenses for the next year. I worked full time and did private duty nursing on my days off and holidays to make extra money. I took over mortgages to save the family farm and car from foreclosure proceedings. This was for family survival.

In July 1960, I relocated from Augusta, Georgia to White Plains, New York to complete a 3-month post-graduate course in Psychiatric Nursing since black students did not get this practical experience (white students received this training) as part of their 3-year nurses training in South Carolina. This training was needed to take the South Carolina State Board Nursing licensing examination and to get licensure in other states. This move was an important turning point in my life. I left my old world in the South and entered a new one filled with opportunities.

"For you to compete on the playing field, which is often unleveled, earn an average compensation, and take your career to the next level, you must know the unwritten rules and play by those rules in any organization."

- Indigo Triplett Johnson, "Playing by the Unwritten Rules--Moving from the middle to the top" (2006 page 1).

LESSONS LEARNED

A recurring theme in my life that has proved beneficial to me– taking on leadership and proactive roles, even though this was discouraged in nursing school.

The importance of always working towards self-improvement cannot be overemphasized.

Think about the "economics" of your decision when picking a career. Choose those that are in demand and have stability. Remember once you have established yourself and have some financial stability—you can look at ways to work towards other pursuits. You need to have a foundation to work from first.

Responsibility to family and friends is an important aspect of life. Don't shirk them—doing the right thing shows strength of character.

Chapter Three ~ Hospital Nurse

"South & North—A World of Difference"

My first nursing job after completing nursing school required me to adjust to a new world. I was now accountable and responsible for patients' lives and well-being. I no longer had the protection of school and nurse instructors. For some people that might have been cause to become scared or hesitant and unsure of themselves. I viewed it like this. I've studied hard to get here, I'll study harder and learn even more now that I'm a practicing nurse and I will not let my patients down. It is that way with good nurses and I knew no matter what, I was a good nurse.

I also believe that it is or should be like that in all professions and for all that a person does in life. You have to step up—don't wait on someone else to hold you accountable—hold yourself responsible for what you do, or what you don't do.

"You only have to do a very few things right in your life, so long as you don't do too many things wrong."

- Warren Buffett

Success in life depends on doing the right things more than doing the wrong things—it's a simple belief I have. It's good to hear that people such as Warren Buffett believe that too.

In spite of the challenges of orientation to the hospital and the seriousness of the responsibilities I now had, I was ecstatic to have a job making $300.00 a month. There was a shortage of nurses, so I had the opportunity to work many hours of overtime or do private duty nursing. I could earn additional money to help my parents and siblings financially and that made me very happy because I believe that family—not self—comes first. There is a balance, that you need in life but if you are able to help, then you should. The extra money and ability to help my family gave me a sense of empowerment and knowledge that I could and did make a difference not only in my life, but also in the life of others.

There is something about that feeling that is both sobering and that frees your thinking. You are no longer bound by considerations of just yourself— your mind is opened up and presented a much bigger picture of the world around you. It's not that you are responsible for the well-being of that world or that you have to try to do every thing for every one. It is not that at all. It is simply you understand that even with the small things and limited number of people that perhaps you can only affect; if you do in a positive way, that they in turn might influence others similarly or go on to do good or even great things. All because in some small way you helped them or were a positive influence. The ripples from that can travel thousands of miles, spread throughout the years and create that truest, purest most wholesome legacy that anyone could ever hope for.

I was proud to be a registered nurse in that starched white uniform and cap ready to help others, including my family. To help comfort another person made me feel wonderful, whether it was giving them something to help relieve their pain or other medications, bathing, feeding, helping them to walk, giving a back rub for comfort or spending time just listening (really listening) to the patient's concerns. That is how it is when your work is not just "work" ... it's something more than just a vocation. It's part of your identity.

* * *

It was a cultural shock relocating from Augusta, GA to White Plains, NY. It was a very different world compared to what I was used to having never been out of the South.

I was admitted as a student to the White Plains Psychiatric Institution for a 3-month postgraduate course in psychiatric nursing as needed for licensure as a registered nurse in most states. The setting and environment were very different, mainly middle and upper income residents, many foreign born. Most of the patients were white and wealthy. This new experience inspired me to stay in New York instead of returning to the South. I felt I had more opportunity in the North and certainly being exposed to people different than what I was accustomed to would stretch my thinking and allow me to network in a way I never could have in the South. This would help me become an even better person for the experience.

I immediately found many nursing positions and an opportunity to return to school for a graduate degree. On completing the psychiatric nursing course, I accepted a position at New York Hospital in New York City with super benefits and a great salary. I relocated to New York City and lived in the New York Hospital housing. This was another milestone in my life—touring famous sites I'd only read or heard about or seen in movies, going to jazz concerts, shopping, going to shows at Radio City Music Hall, the wonderful restaurants, operas and plays to go to. And I loved the hustle and bustle of the stock market—it was busy but also had an organization to it ... a pattern to the way it worked that I got a tremendous charge from. I felt like a plant must feel when it is finally watered and freshens and blossoms. I truly knew I was at the world's doorstep and had just been invited in! It was a fabulous experience, which I thoroughly enjoyed. I had many family members and friends constantly visiting me in New York and I became an expert tour guide.

At the hospital, there were bright and energetic medical and nursing students eager to learn. I had the opportunity to work with them and their faculty members. I was a staff nurse, quickly moved up to assistant, and then head nurse. That sounds great and things just fell into place for me but it wasn't quite that simple. I believe firmly that a strong work ethic and interest in furthering yourself does more for your chances of success than any amount of passive "wishing and dreaming." I worked all the hours I could, which not only made me more money but also accelerated my level of experience. I learned more and faster ... by doing more and reaching for new things to learn and do. I approached everything I did then, and still do now with basic common sense to do my job responsibly. To be on time, never shirk and when new opportunities came from that approach take them on with willingness to try as hard as I could and not accept mediocrity.

"The secret of success is to do the common things uncommonly well."

\- John D. Rockefeller

After one year at the hospital, I met two nurses whom were in the New York Air National Guard as flight nurses. They invited me to visit Floyd Bennett Field Air National Guard Base to check out the opportunities to fly. I had never forgotten that moment in the cotton field, watching the airplane cut a swath through the sky—far and away from toiling in the hot fields. From that day, it seemed everything I'd done, planned and worked towards and for, had led me to where I was at that point in time. The right place and time to meet two people that I never would have met otherwise. I still keep in touch with one of them and our friendship over the years, along with many others equally as long, shows that the continuity and consistency of relations are very important to your quality of life and plays a role in anchoring you in a way that a more transient relationship style might never accomplish.

That visit to the airfield significantly affected the rest of my life. Talking with my two new friends about their experience and a chance conversation with a Tech Sergeant who shared with me his thoughts on how his service in the Air National Guard benefited him, helped me make the decision to join the New York Air National Guard as a commissioned officer and enter Flight Nurse training. That decision led me to seek an Air Force career and to pursue a graduate degree.

You can feel the transition moment when a jet has kicked in the afterburners or as a pilot; you push forward on the throttles and feel the vibration and surge. When I made the decision to join the Air National Guard and to pursue becoming a Flight Nurse, I felt the same way. I had now entered another new world and stage in my life.

"We are defined more by what we don't know about ourselves, than by what we do know. Change offers us the chance to discover what we don't know and therefore helps us reach our potential."

- Mimi Welch

From this point on, my civilian and military careers paralleled—each would be marked and milestones reached with a steady progression of new positions, advancing education, new responsibilities and new rewards.

LESSONS LEARNED

How leaving what is "known" behind you to start something new, in a place you may have never been before—can be a good thing. It promotes self-reliance and simply that is probably one of the most powerful things a young person can learn and have.

The importance of being responsible for your own actions cannot be understated.

Whatever your job is, reach out to learn more. Stretch yourself to learn beyond your job description. When you do that, life rewards you with opportunities that you may not receive otherwise.

Chapter Four ~ Military & Civilian Careers

Flight Nurse

Ten years after that day in 1954, where I stood in the cotton field, watching that plane climb high in the sky; I proudly walked upon the stage and accepted my silver flight nurse wings at the Aerospace School of Medicine, Flight Nurse Branch, Brooks Air Force Base, San Antonio, Texas. This is one of my most cherished accomplishments!

In a way, it was the end of the beginning for me and the start of the rest of my life.

This new stage of my life called for me to place even more emphasis on a combination of realism and idealism. I'd chosen nursing because I knew that I would always be able to find a job. Though my reason to join the Air National Guard was partly due to my desire to fulfill my dream of flying; that came from my heart. What I knew in my head was that a career in the military because its rules to some extent protected even further against discrimination, coupled with the demand for nurses (and flight nurses specifically) was a powerful combination and foundation for me to excel in both careers. I felt there would also be increasing improvement in women's rights throughout the sixties and early seventies. And that they would lead to changes in the military that would result in opportunities for women who had established themselves in the service.

In 1974, Congress required the Armed Services to drop its 2 percent cap on women in the military. Bringing more women into the military created a demand for leadership by those of us already in service. Long-term, my thinking had proved correct, as I had positioned myself to take on roles of increasing rank and responsibility in both my military and civilian careers.

* * *

In April 1963, at Floyd Bennett Field in Brooklyn, New York I was commissioned as a First Lieutenant in the New York Air National Guard. I attended Basic Officer Orientation in October 1963 and subsequently enrolled in the Aerospace 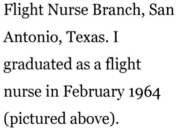 School of Medicine, Flight Nurse Branch, San Antonio, Texas. I

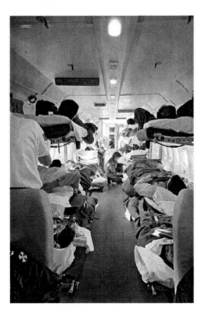

graduated as a flight nurse in February 1964 (pictured above).

A Flight Nurse requires specialized training on how to care

for patients at altitude. Bodies and medications react differently at high altitudes and different air pressure. There were also specific protocols required in the care of military personnel, their families and diplomats during national and international flights. During a transport, the nurse is the senior medical person on the plane. Along with the medical team, you decide who goes on the plane and who doesn't. It is very important to make that judgment properly.

It took me many years of experience to progress in my career and to work towards and receive advanced college degrees. I was always willing to work for what I wanted. I did not have a sense of entitlement nor a need for instant gratification—I knew that as long as I broke what I needed to do down into manageable chunks, that one step at a time, I could get to wherever I decided I needed to go.

My commissioning in the New York Air National Guard (ANG) as a First Lieutenant was a key event in my life. I met many nice and highly motivated ANG members—the type of colleagues and peers that drive you to be the best you can be. It was a perfect setting for me.

Basic Officer Orientation was like an electric shock physically and mentally, however I quickly adjusted to the rigor: structure, studying policy and regulations orders and the marching. I actually came to love the new environment, the disciplined regimen and most importantly, the wonderful and bright doctors, dentists, nurses and other professionals.

Flight Nurse School was very challenging, but inspiring. I had to learn nursing and reactions of various diseases from ground to the flight environment and pressurized aircraft. It was very different from nursing on the ground. The flight emergency training and procedures were scary, especially the training for trouble over water or "ditching" at sea. I really did not like flying over deep water early in my career.

* * *

"An Unexpected Crash"

In most plane crashes, you have some warning that the plane is in trouble—and even if only a minute or two—you still have those moments to prepare your thoughts, brace for impact etc. In my life, I've flown hundreds of times and on many types of aircraft—the only crash I was involved in was very unexpected. A few months after receiving my flight nurse wings in 1964, I was onboard a C-97, that crashed while landing in Charleston, South Carolina. Though onboard the aircraft, I learned the exact details after the crash was investigated and written up.

C-97 Stratofreighter

This was my first cross-country flight after completing flight nurse school. We left Floyd Bennett Field in Brooklyn, New York on a Friday evening traveling to San Juan, Puerto with a stop at Charleston AFB, SC to pick-up passengers. The weather was clear with no clouds as we headed to SC.

We were on a scheduled training mission and just completing the first leg with the landing in Charleston. We were landing in the dark, the forecast called for Visual Flight Rules (VFR), and there was a gentle breeze from the east. We had completed our Aeromedical Evacuation Training, took a short coffee break and buckled in for the landing.

Following is the crash report:

We descended from 8,000 to 5,000 and then down to 1,500. Local Approach Control provided radar vectors to the VOR final course for landing. During the drop to approach altitude, the copilot was busy on the radios. The aircraft commander (AC) reached over him to change the flap positions three times. He called "RPM 2350, gear down before landing check list." The copilot acknowledged this request and read off "Engine RPM 2350," and "Landing Gear Down." The flight engineer heard someone report that a visual gear check was completed, and passed that on to the pilots. The AC requested two more flap changes, which the copilot made.

Upon hearing the "gear down" request, a crewmember (called a scanner) looked out at the left main gear and decided that it was down. He then moved to the across the aircraft to help another crewmember who could not see the right main gear.

When the flight engineer switched on the wheel well lights, the nose gear cursorily checked as being down, and the right gear was again checked. Since no light was visible, the junior scanner headed to the cockpit to inform the flight engineer of the problem. He arrived just in time to see the approach lights disappear, and felt the aircraft hit the runway. The other scanner meanwhile had decided to recheck the left gear, and discovered it was up. Moving fast to the cockpit, he'd just opened the cockpit door, when the aircraft props started striking the runway.

All three landing gear, left, nose and right, was still up and locked. They had not been lowered though the gear switch was in the down position. The landing was very rough as the aircraft struck the ground; lights went out, the commander immediately ordered, "abandon ship" as we quickly checked to make sure no one was still in the aircraft. A check of all systems did not find any problems. It is hard to see landing gear when it is dark, especially if the wheel well lights aren't working and the indicator lights used at that time could be misinterpreted. But it was clear that the copilot had not lowered the landing gear when requested by the AC.

* * *

C-97

The C-97 was a double-decker type airplane and we walked quickly over the wing to the ground and ran a distance in case the airplane exploded or caught fire due to full fuel tanks. Fire trucks, emergency vehicles and security police appeared immediately to take us to a building to safety after determining that we were not injured.

We were questioned extensively about weather, what we observed, heard and experienced from the time we left New York and at landing in Charleston. I was asked if I was considering not flying again. I said *"absolutely not"* and went on flying the next day with a replacement aircraft. Even though we all were "shaken," and were very happy to be alive; I was thinking to my self—I really did not intend to spend time and energy earning silver  wings just to be killed and get them bloody. Even though I had very few material things, I had a car and life insurance. I quickly consulted legal advice and completed a will. At that point, I surmised that I was saved from death for a reason. I must complete my mission even though I did not have a clue yet what that divine assignment was.

There were 19 people on the airplane, 2 women and 17 men; however, the Charleston, SC newspaper described the crash of an Air National Guard airplane with 19 men onboard. Of interest, my parents lived just over 120 from Charleston and read about the crash in the newspaper, but they were not aware that I was involved in the crash.

I'm sure that what happened in that crash resulted in a harsh lesson for some, and changes and more strict discipline for landing procedures for all flight crews. There are also some things that I took from this on a personal level that you the reader should know that I touch on at the end of this chapter.

I remained on flying status accumulating hundreds of hours over nearly twelve years as a flight nurse, flight nurse instructor and flight nurse examiner traveling all over the world. Through hard work and determination, I advanced quickly in the ranks, earning promotion to flight nurse instructor in 1966, flight nurse examiner in 1968

(pictured on the right) and to chief nurse a few years later. It appeared with

my choice to become a nurse and then join the Air National Guard—that in spite of different challenges and barriers, many great opportunities were offered to me. It seems that I constantly was at the right place at the right time.

In October 1993, almost 30-years after receiving my wings, I received my first star and was selected to become the first female  African-American general in the 359-year history of the National Guard, the military's oldest branch of our armed forces.

 I was promoted to Major General in September 1998 (pinning ceremony pictured at left), I retired with that rank in September 29, 2001 after serving in the Air Force and Air National Guard for 38 years, 5 months, 26 days and 3 hours.

Over that 38-year period I had the opportunity to serve my country as not only a flight nurse but also as a nurse examiner, chief nurse executive, commander, advisor to the Chief, Air Force Nurse

Corps, for Readiness and Nursing Services, Office of the Surgeon General, and Assistant to the Director, Air National Guard for Human Resources Readiness.

All the while, I never stopped learning, graduating cum laude with a bachelor's degree from Jersey City State College in 1971. I earned a master's degree in public health from Yale University in 1973 and a doctorate in health education from Columbia University in 1983.

* * *

My "Olympic" Moment

There were numerous opportunities to serve and participate in unique assignments with the Air Force and Air National Guard.

During part of February and March 1980 (while I was a Major assigned to 105th TAC Medical Clinic NYANG, White Plains, NY) I participated along with a select group of New York Militia personnel on State

active duty as a member of the Poly Olympic Medical Clinic in support of the 1980 Winter Olympics in Lake Placid, New York.

This duty was in support of the International Olympic Committee's demanding accomplishment expressed as "Welcome World...We're Ready!"

Baron Pierre de Coubertin, the founder of the modern Olympic Games adopted the symbol of five interlocking rings on the Olympic Flag from a stone alter which is still standing at Delphi, in Greece. They represent the uniting of the five continents. The Flag of every nation in the world has at least one of the five rings colors. The white background symbolizes purity.

The Olympics is an organization whose beliefs about the spirit of effort, of discipline and representation of your national and individual identity largely mirrored my own.

The event was a world-class international experience with numerous opportunities to network, use clinical medical skills, and enhance personal and professional development skills. The weather was extremely cold, reaching temperatures 70 below zero with strong winds at intervals. We had an opportunity to meet and observe many of the Olympic athletes in action. A truly memorable event in my life.

* * *

Commanding the 105th TAC Medical Clinic

As the chief nurse executive for the 105th TAC Medical Clinic, in 1986 I was asked by my commanding officer, the group commander (GC) Major General Paul Weaver, Jr., to make two recommendations for qualified officers to take command of the medical clinic. Which I did—submitting to him the two best-qualified officers based on my experience and in my judgment. The result of my recommendations was unexpected.

General Weaver told me, "Here I am, with you following orders, doing your job by recommending suitable officers to take command of the clinic—when it hit me—the best candidate is right in front of me."

When General Weaver offered me the command, I was totally in "shock." A command of this type historically went to white male physicians. No females had ever commanded a clinic or hospital unit—for him to offer the command to me, an African American woman, no matter how well qualified—was a startling thing! Nationally, there were some unhappy medical personnel due to this decision, which ultimately benefited many other professionals such as nurses, dentists, biomedical service corps and other medical service corps officers. This decision opened the door to those whom would not have had an opportunity to serve as a commander. The GC had the support of the senior officials of the National

Guard at the Pentagon. And in 1986, I was appointed commander of the 105th USAF Medical Clinic in Newburgh, N.Y. I was the first Air National Guard nurse to command a medical clinic. I was determined to be successful in the position and was. This success earned me yet another stepping-stone to new opportunities.

* * *

The Major General Irene Trowell-Harris Chapter
of
Tuskegee Airmen, Inc.
A Decade of Mentoring...Accented by Gold

In 1998, I became the first woman to have a Tuskegee Airmen, Inc. Chapter named in my honor—the "Major General Irene Trowell-Harris Chapter" in Newburgh, New York. I talk in depth about this later in the book.

In 1999, a mentoring award was also named in my honor at the 105th Airlift Wing, Newburgh, New York.

I also served as a military representative to DACOWITS. The Defense Department Advisory Committee on Women in the Services (DACOWITS) was established in 1951 by then Secretary of Defense, George C. Marshall. The Committee is composed of civilian women and men appointed by the Secretary of Defense to provide advice and recommendations on matters and policies relating to the recruitment and retention, treatment, employment, integration, and well-being of highly qualified professional women in the Armed Forces.

Beginning in 2002, the Committee began providing advice and recommendations on family issues related to recruitment and retention of a highly qualified professional military. Historically, DACOWITS' recommendations have been very instrumental in effecting changes to laws and policies pertaining to military women.

* * *

Civilian Career

My civilian career has been just as full and rewarding. I have had the opportunity to serve as nurse manager, supervisor, chief nurse executive, university professor, senior policy specialist and Director, Northeast Region, Office of Healthcare Inspections, Office of Inspector General, Department of Veterans Affairs, Washington, DC.

In 1993, I left active duty and chose to come to work for the Department of Veterans Affairs instead of taking a more lucrative job working for a defense contractor. Several people told me there were still issues in the military and veterans systems that needed attention, and I wanted to help fix them.

I had that chance as director of patient care inspections and program evaluation with VA's Office of the Inspector General and later in the IG's office as

VA director of the Washington, D.C., Office of Health Care Inspections. My IG experience was helpful because it gave me skills to immediately identify an issue, generate solutions and follow through to be sure the solutions were implemented.

In 1997, I served as the Air Force speaker representing the United States at the International Conference on Women in Defense in Johannesburg, South Africa. In addition, I was the 1997 Air Force representative for the Committee on Women in the North Atlantic Treaty Organization (NATO) Conference, Istanbul, Turkey.

I was appointed director of the Center for Women Veterans in October 2001, a political appointment from the White House. Congress passed legislation in 1994 authorizing the Department of Veterans Affairs (VA) to establish a Center for Women Veterans. As director, I serve as the primary advisor to Secretary of Veterans Affairs on all matters related to programs, issues, legislation, and initiatives for and affecting women veterans.

As director of the Center for Women Veterans, I work to ensure that female veterans are aware of their benefits and services available to them, including health care, education, counseling, insurance, and home and business loans. Services to female veterans will become increasingly important as the proportion of women in the military increases. Women now constitute 7.5 percent (1.8 million) of the nation's 23.4 million living veterans, and the percentage will increase for two reasons: first, because the number of women in active service has risen, to 17 percent; and second, because male veterans, mostly from World War II, are dying at a rate of 1,400 per day.

LESSONS LEARNED

People and systems are not infallible. It's important to take your responsibilities seriously—even though repetition can lead to complacency or even a slack attitude—don't let it be you that make a mistake.

Don't just think about your own job. Help those around you by making them more aware of the importance of doing their jobs correctly.

Do the very best you can in your job or profession—even though you think that no one cares—you should care! You never know who is observing and making decisions based on your performance.

Appreciate our nation's veterans—help them in any way that you can.

Chapter Five ~ Family

"Never underestimate the importance of family"

Irene Battle Trowell, center, was surrounded children, grandchildren and great-grandchildren during a Friday visit to the Aiken County Historical Museum.

Picture from The Aiken Standard, November 24, 2007

I was born just two generations away from slavery.

My grandfather, Jim Trowell, was enslaved until he was in his early 20s. After the Civil War, a white family took him under its wing, bequeathing him 50 acres in South Carolina that my parents gradually enlarged into a 200-acre farm. I was born in that farmhouse in 1939.

There have been good times and bad times in my life and in my family's lives. However, in the bad times I am reminded of this line from a poem, which inspired new hope in many Black Americans:

> *"History, despite its wrenching pain, cannot be unlived; but if faced with courage, need not be lived again."*

> \- Maya Angelou

My parents came from humble beginnings; they did not have health insurance, indoor plumbing, a bank account, or any of the material things that signify the "American Dream." But they had unconditional love and an insatiable desire to help their children become successful in life with a good religious foundation and education.

Since our parents mainly worked on the farm, they both retired with very small social security income. All the siblings contributed to our parents through their life usually starting in high school. Some lived near and visited frequently, helped on the farm, assisted with their care, shopped for them, some gave money at intervals and one brother built them a new 3-bed room house. After completing nursing school, living away from home and learning about life in general, I knew I had to help improve the family situation to help them with health insurance, money to continue my siblings' education, upgrade plumbing, open bank accounts and participate in recreation such as travel and social events. The first step was to send my parents a check monthly to help cover the usual household bills such as health and life insurance, clothing, heating fuel, car and farm equipment maintenance.

I graduated from nursing school on 2 Sep 59 and went to work the following Monday at Talmadge Hospital in Augusta, Georgia with a salary of $300 per month. When I received my first check in October 1959, I was ecstatic. I sent my parents a check monthly from October 1959, for almost fifty years, until their deaths, my father in September 1998 and mother until her death in January 2008. She died prior to signing her last check. When I was traveling overseas, I would send them the checks pre-dated with a note to wait until the second of the month to cash or deposit the check.

In spite of my parents' situation, they tried to provide for and plan the family future when possible as related to education, weddings, farm work, planting gardens, shopping, recreation activities and visiting relatives.

Let me tell you an example of preparing for the future. My mother passed away in January 2008 and she was aware that she would be transitioning to another level of life at some point. She planned well for her journey. Over 15 years before her death, in August 1993 she selected her coffin including the color and model number—to make sure we got it right, she specified that she wanted to be buried in her white usher uniform with her Union Progress Society pin, and she even selected the color of her flowers.

A few years before passing, she divided her property among the children because she did want any disagreements after her death. She told us that her bags were packed and she was well prepared for her journey because her work on earth was done. Upon her death at age 90, the family requested that in lieu of flowers donations be made to the Aiken County Historical Museum for education of students about history. The museum established the Irene Battle Trowell Memorial Education Fund in her honor. The purpose of this fund is to educate children at all grade levels in the county and contiguous areas on history. Children get an opportunity to go to the museum and experience history including military and veterans' history. The museum displayed a family exhibit for a few months of four generations of Trowell family with photographs and a wall scroll of the families.

As a family, we celebrate births, marriages, weddings, graduations, promotions, retirements, family reunions, even deaths. When my mother passed away, she requested that we celebrate her life's work of dedication to family, community and church.

She and my father raised their own eleven children and seventeen special needs children. Those children that usually no one wanted to care for. She also served in her church for over seventy years in various positions as Society secretary, teacher, usher and housemother. Family values, unity and support from the entire community clearly empowered her children to become successful. It truly does take a village.

* * *

It was not enough for me to complete nursing school and consider myself successful with silver flight nurse wings. My success was not something that I felt I should "save" for myself. I knew that I must share it with my family. I immediately assisted my sisters and brothers with emotional and financial support for college and business ventures. Investing in the human potential of my brothers and sisters really paid off for the family.

It was not just about giving or loaning my family money. It was also about my new life and where I lived, becoming somewhat of a venue and opportunity for my siblings to come north to discover their own opportunities while having me as a resource to help them.

My sister Mae came to live with me in New York City after completing high school. She worked as an Operator at the New York Telephone Company and at New York Hospital as a Ward Clerk for two years prior to deciding to attend nursing school. With my support, she graduated from Harlem Hospital School of Nursing with honors in Gynecological Nursing and practiced for 30 years as a nurse in Queens, New York, retiring January 2003, as associate director of nursing with the New York Health and Hospital Corporation. She and her spouse purchased a house in Tampa, Florida and relocated there in 2004.

The next sibling to live with me for a short while was my brother Jack who worked at the New York Times in the newspaper morgue. He also sold magazines door-to-door during the summer to earn additional money. One day after being chased by several ferocious dogs, he quickly gave up selling magazines. This is when Jack decided to attend college rather than working at menial jobs. During this time in New York, we enjoyed the summer by attending theaters, Radio City Music Hall shows, sightseeing tours and smorgasbords. We checked out every smorgasbord in New York City since my brother loved to eat and ate what seemed like tons of food. That summer I took Jack on his first airplane ride with American Airlines during an open house at LaGuardia Airport in New York.

Jack returned to Aiken, South Carolina, applied to several colleges and was admitted in August 1966 to the biology pre-medical program at Claflin University in Orangeburg, South Carolina. When he received his acceptance notice, he called me because he did not have tuition for college. After working for a few years and assisting my parents financially, I only had $1,400 in my savings account. Jack said that he needed $1,200 in order to start school. I withdrew the $1,200 from my savings account and sent Jack the money for college. However, I did threaten his life that if he *"wasted my hard earned money I would do him bodily harm."*

Jack entered college and did very well academically. He subsequently transferred in his junior year to Howard University in Washington, DC and graduated in May 1970. He was admitted to the Howard University Medical School in the fall of 1970 and graduated in May 1974 with a Doctor of Medicine (MD). (Jack had planned to become a farmer, raising chickens as he had done during his time in high school where he won several awards for prize chickens.) After completing medical school, Jack joined the United States Air Force and completed subspecialty training on an Air Force Fellowship in Gastroenterology. He served on active duty as a Major and Chief, Division of Gastroenterology, Department of Medicine, Malcolm Grow USAF Medical Center, Andrews Air Force Base, Maryland. He subsequently served in the Air Force Reserve and as a flight surgeon in the New York Air National Guard.

The next sibling to attend school was my brother Lafayette who graduated from Aiken High School (an integrated school) in 1973. He was accepted and attended Embry-Riddle Aeronautical

University in Daytona, Florida for pilot training. I traveled from New York to Aiken, South Carolina to accompany Lafayette to college since this was a new experience for him and his first major travel event. Flight training was very expensive since Lafayette did not have a scholarship. I paid several thousand dollars during the year for his tuition. At that time, I was working in New York as a head/nurse manager and on flying status with the New York Air National Guard. Even with two jobs and overtime at the hospital intervals, it was challenging since Jack was in medical school and Lafayette in pilot training during the same period. Lafayette was an honor student and graduated with his wings. He subsequently served as flight instructor at Embry-Riddle prior to establishing his very successful satellite electronic and TV business back in Aiken.

Other siblings Lee, Crey, Franklin and Sherry Diane pursued small business ventures or careers such as in long-distance trucking, landscaping, construction, cement finishing, law enforcement and satellite electronics. They all still reside in Aiken.

Frances lives in Queens, NY, pursued law enforcement as her career and is retired from the NYC police department.

In spite of the many great events in my life with family, some deaths affected me profoundly. The loss of my friend and mentor Dr. Jack Trowell in July 1993; my father, Frank the "wheel man" in September 1998; my mother, Irene Battle the family icon in January 2008 and my brother Lee (pictured below on the left with his wife and two of his four daughters), my best friend and confidant in October 2009. For me the final act of death cannot be accurately

described psychologically in words. However, we can recognize the dead by honoring their memory and by taking care of the living.

Family does not just end with parents and siblings though. I've helped 14 of my 32 nieces and nephews obtain scholarships and pay for college. At the family reunions, I helped organize every three years, I tell them to stay in touch, to keep their lives in balance and to keep learning. I advise them *"to turn obstacles into stepping-stones"* and that persistence pays off.

One story I share with them illustrates this: early in my career in the Air National Guard, a chief nurse warned me that I'd never make it past Major, "no matter how good I was". I just thanked her and said 'OK'. I went four ranks beyond Major, to Major General. That is a better response than any I could ever have given her.

LESSONS LEARNED

Family first. Invest in the potential of your family. Help them if you are able to.

Just because someone says, "you'll never make it" doesn't mean that is so. You control your destiny. If you want to get somewhere bad enough—you'll figure ways to get there.

Value and enjoy family members every day!

Chapter Six ~ Tuskegee Airmen Inc.

"The 'Red Tails' and What They Meant"

This chapter is not about me but is about something and a group of men I'm very proud of. It touches on something that people of all races and ethnic backgrounds should wish to emulate and certainly must respect.

There is a recurring theme in the background of some of the most successful people in all areas of human endeavors. Adversity and overcoming it. They overcame the challenges, the obstacles and the barriers that they were faced with. That above all deserves honor and respect.

In the dark, early days of World War II, there was a group of men that individually and collectively faced everything that centuries old racist thinking and stereotyping could throw at them—just so they could fight for the very country that thought them incapable.

It took the United States Congress in 1941 to force the Army Air Corps to form an African American combat unit. On March 19, 1941, the 99th Pursuit Squadron ("Pursuit" being the pre-World War II term for what would become "Fighter") was activated, which in turn became the core to form other

squadrons.

In June 1941, the Tuskegee program officially began with formation of the 99th Fighter Squadron at the Tuskegee Institute. The War Department's efforts to derail the formation of the combat unit consisted of establishing very high requirements for higher education and flight experience. They felt safe since they did not believe any African American men would be able to meet those requirements. The Tuskegee Institute had participated in the Civilian Pilot Training Program

since 1939 and many African American men had
taken part in it. Thanks to the quality of the education
and training program at the Tuskegee Institute, the
War Department's plan backfired when the Air Corps
received more than enough applications from men
who qualified—meeting the high bar of entry.

The Tuskegee
Airmen story is about
men who rose above
adversity and
discrimination and
opened a door once
closed to black America.
Before the Tuskegee

Airmen, no African American combat units or military
pilots existed. The Tuskegee Airmen went on to serve
honorably throughout WWII becoming one of its most
highly decorated units.

Today there are 50 chapters of the Tuskegee
Airmen, Inc. (TAI) that honor the memory of the
Tuskegee Airmen and what they stood for.

Chaplain (Lt Col) Julius Jefferson of the 105th Airlift Wing, a former Stewart Air National Guard Base member, went to the Tuskegee Airmen, Inc. (TAI) convention in Kansas City and was so inspired that he asked about forming a chapter at Stewart Air National Guard Base (ANGB). The Stewart chapter of TAI was named in my honor and that recognition humbles me. The Major General Irene Trowell-Harris Chapter of TAI was organized on January 10, 1998 at Stewart Air National Guard Base in Newburgh, New York.

The chapter was named for me based on my accomplishments as the first African American female two-star general in 359-year history of the Guard and the first female and nurse in Air National Guard history to command a medical clinic. But I could not have accomplished some of the things I did while in the military if the Tuskegee Airmen had not blazed a trail for me by their efforts and desire to fight for their country, and then by excelling once they were able to.

I would like to share with you some of what the mission of Tuskegee Airmen, Inc. (TAI) is:

- To foster recognition of, and preserve the history of African-American achievement in aviation.

- To inspire and motivate young men and women toward endeavors in aviation and aerospace careers. In essence, to mentor and build bridges for young students nationally.

- To bring together in a spirit of friendship and goodwill, all persons who share in the aspirations and successes of men and women who pioneered in military aviation and in the Tuskegee experiment.

In addition, TAI National programs:

- Administer youth aviation programs

- Provide mentors and role models

- Perform community outreach and mentoring

- Make nominations to service academies

- Do historical research

Specifically my namesake Chapter's goals are:

- To promote the interests and honor the memories of the men and women who served in the Army Air Corps at Tuskegee Alabama during the 1940s.

- To continue to provide financial assistance to the National Scholarship Fund and the Historic Museum Fund.

- To continue to sponsor the Annual Major General Irene Trowell-Harris Chapter Tuition Assistance Award Celebration; this provides scholarships to local college-bound students.

- To become one of the leading Tuskegee Airmen Chapters by providing positive and ambitious mentors to young men and women.

- To create a pilot enrichment program; this will expose students to the aviation career field.

In pursuit of these goals, the chapter will continue to forge partnerships with community leaders who possess information and knowledge consistent with chapter goals. The chapter realizes that the local community is imperative to the organization's progress.

The Lee A. Archer, Jr. Red Tail Youth Flying Program was started on October 6, 2001. This program provides instruction and mentoring primarily low to middle-income youth that would not normally have the opportunity to attend flight school or have an aviation mentor. We are proud of this one of a kind program that gives students an opportunity to receive their private pilot licenses, as they become seniors in high school.

The chapter hosts the Annual Willie Carter Golf Classic. Willie Carter is a local golf pro who has been touching the lives of many people through his golf clinics, schools and pro shop. He is a former principal at a local elementary school and is a businessman. He was selected as the recipient of the Major General Irene Trowell-Harris Chapter of Tuskegee Airmen,

Inc. Community mentoring award for his work with youth and the community.

The chapter hosts a dinner annually in February to award scholarships and help sponsor a family day during the summer in Newburgh, NY. We will continue to build on the successes of these and other programs to make the Trowell-Harris chapter the premier chapter of Tuskegee Airmen, Inc.

In addition, the Chapter will continually promote the rich history of the Tuskegee Airmen and honor those "Red Tails" still among us. Whether during chapter-sponsored functions or in everyday activities as chapter members, we will herald the outstanding achievements and spirit of the Tuskegee Airmen.

MG Irene Trowell-Harris Chapter,

Tuskegee Airmen, Inc.

One Maguire Way

Stewart ANGB

Newburgh, NY 12550-5076

Tel: (845) 838-7848

Fax: (845) 567-1731

Email: TAI_NY@hotmail.com

www.TAI-NY.org

Chapter Seven ~ What I Believe

"Believing in your self is critical for success"

As a child, I followed the way my parents brought me and my brothers and sisters up.

- They did it with love.

- They did it with respect.

- They did it with a willingness to undertake hard work because it was what was needed to be done for the family.

I learned when you come from not having anything, when you finally have something it is truly a blessing.

Coming up that way has created in me an appreciation of things and people; an appreciation that I hope I never lose or take for granted. I like and admire the finer things in life, but I've never chased them or felt that I needed them to be happy.

The best gift that you can give to yourself is to truly understand as soon as possible in life, what it is that makes you happy—and then make that your life's focus. But not to the exclusion of everything else, because in all things we need balance.

You have to have a centerpiece to build your life around, or perhaps better said ... a compass that keeps you pointed in the right direction. Life buffets you. At times, it can be a harsh wind blowing from all corners. Without something within you to give you strength to bear the winds and to keep your equilibrium, you never know what direction you should go in, and can fall, never to get up.

I'm a deeply spiritual person but one that does not need to evangelize. I prefer quiet strength to loud superficiality where talking is just for talking's sake. Our world that seems to gravitate towards sound bites and short attention spans is often mesmerized by flash and show. I believe that a life of value comes from a willingness to slow things down, to be someone of substance (and no I do not mean substance by way of material things), by taking time to consider things before making decisions, speaking out or responding. To take time to understand ourselves is far more important than time spent puzzling over the meaning of "everyone else."

"You are accountable for your own successes and failures."

- Indigo Triplett Johnson, "Playing by the Unwritten Rules--Moving from the middle to the top" (2006 page 92).

Following is something written more than a hundred years ago that is ageless in its wisdom. It was written in another time so where it refers to "men," "man" and "son" understand that it equally applies to women and daughters.

If you can keep your head when all about you

Are losing theirs and blaming it on you;

If you can trust yourself when all men doubt you

But make allowance for their doubting too;

If you can wait and not be tired by waiting,

Or being lied about, don't deal in lies;

Or being hated don't give way to hating,

And yet don't look too good, nor talk too wise;

If you can dream – and not make dreams your
master;

If you can think – and not make thoughts your aim,

If you can meet with Triumph and Disaster,

And treat those two impostors just the same;

If you can bear to hear the truth you've spoken

Twisted by knaves to make a trap for fools;

Or watch the things you gave your life to, broken

And stoop and build them up with worn-out tools;

If you can make one heap of all your winnings

And risk it on one turn of pitch-and-toss,

And lose, and start again at your beginnings,

And never breathe a word about your loss;

If you can force your heart and nerve and sinew

To serve your turn long after they are gone,

And so hold on when there is nothing in you

Except the will, which says to them "Hold On"

If you can talk with crowds and keep your virtue,

Or walk with kings – nor lose the common touch;

If neither foes nor loving friends can hurt you,

If all men count with you, but none too much;

If you can fill the unforgiving minute

With sixty seconds worth of distance run,

Yours is the Earth and all that is in it,

And – which is more you will be a man, my son.

- Rudyard Kipling

I've lived a life that has encountered everything that Kipling's poem "If" covered. I believe in everything it says. And the advice he gives his readers is advice I would give to anyone and specifically to you, the reader of this book. In those words is a "gift" of wisdom that if you take that away from your reading of this book—then I in turn have received a "gift" from you.

Surely, the world would be a better place if all men and women had more confidence within themselves to treat fairly with each other and with the circumstances of their lives.

I believe that if we opened our hearts to speak, we would find that "minds" shaped by what the hearts have to say, have more in common than we have in differences.

As a young child, I believed in faith, faith in God and in myself. Those simple beliefs built on the foundation of what my parents instilled in me—that I believe in still to this day—have carried me a very long way from my roots in South Carolina.

As a leader, I was educated to inspire, share, and mentor others along the way. You see earning silver wings, two stars, degrees, a doctorate and becoming a White House political appointee is not enough. These accomplishments must be used to benefit our nation and our society, specifically, young people, families and communities.

In retrospect, I believe that I was touched by an angel in that South Carolina cotton field. I did not know it at the time but I was given a mission, not only to become a nurse in order to help others, to advance the profession, to serve this great nation, but I was also given an ambassador role to inspire others to achieve and reach their goals.

I believe that we are placed on earth for a special purpose. Even though our role at times may not be clear to us, we are obligated to do our best with our God given talents.

Even though I realized my dream, like many others, I have had my share of challenges, obstacles and disappointments. Just like others, I did house work, and worked outside the home (along with farm work, I delivered newspapers and as a teenager worked in fast food restaurants) to supplement family income. I dealt with the hard things you need to do in order to succeed.

Your soul comes alive when you believe that and have the determination to follow a dream, to create change, to do what is right over what is easy, and the courage to value tomorrow as much or more as you do today. Eleanor Roosevelt stated this point succinctly when she said:

"The future belongs to those who believe in the beauty of their dreams."

* * *

One question I've been asked is how can we systematically help the masses of young women and men in order to inspire them to reach their potential.

I know that we must care about young people because they are our future leaders. Dr. Martin Luther King said that we must care about each other because:

"We are bound together in an inescapable network of mutuality, tied in a single garment of destiny. Whatever affects one directly affects all indirectly."

To answer, in part, the question posed above, this is what I tell students and young people I speak to:

Apply your self, stay focused, be positive, seek opportunities, then spread your wings and soar like an eagle to greater heights. In order to become successful and to stay successful—you must remain vigilant and never give up:

- If I had given up on my dream to fly, I would not have the silver wings I earned and wore for 38-years.

- If I had given up when I was told I would never progress beyond the rank of Major, I would not have earned the two stars of a Major General.

- If I had given up when I was denied admission to the first nursing school to which I applied, I would not have a master's degree from Yale and a doctorate from Columbia.

- If I had given up when my doctoral committee drilled me for hours; I would not have been inducted into the Teachers College, Columbia University Nursing Hall of Fame.

- If I had given up, I would not have been honored by the Department of Epidemiology and Public Health (EPH), Yale University School of Medicine, for outstanding dedication to public service and inducted into the EPH Public Service Honor Roll.

- If I had given up on my professional goals, I would not have received the Dr. James D. Weaver Alumni Society award.

This is what I believe and the advice I have for Young People, whether you are beginning your career, advancing your career or looking for a career change:

First, you must take care of yourself and maintain a balance, that is physically, mentally, socially, economically, politically and spiritually (don't forget to pray) beneficial to you.

Second, in order to become successful, you must get a good education. Education was the hope of the past and it is surely the hope for the future. Education is a tool that empowers people to be better performers, communicators, supervisors, managers, and citizens. Education is the great liberator! Remember education is a journey, NOT a destination.

Third, do your very best in the job that you have. You may not be able to change the world, but you can shine a light where you are!

Fourth, you must visualize the future and dare to be a part of it! Say to your self *"my contributions are important and I will be a part of this great nation's future."*

* * *

Spiritual Growth—a challenge of today's world

To grow spiritually in a world defined by power, money, and influence can be a monumental effort.

Today's modern conveniences such as electronic equipment, iPhones, iPods, cell phones, gadgets, and tools as well as entertainment through television, magazines, and the web have predisposed us to confine our attention mostly to physical needs and wants.

As a result, our concepts of self-worth and self-meaning can often be muddled and confused. How can we strike a balance between the material (which is increasingly demanding) and spiritual (often over looked) aspects of our lives?

To grow spiritually is to search for meaning to our lives. Religions that believe in the existence of God such as Christianity, Judaism, and Islam suppose that the purpose of the human life is to serve the Creator of all things. Several theories in psychology propose that we ultimately give meaning to our own lives.

Whether we believe that life's meaning is predetermined or self-directed, to grow in spirit is to realize that we do not merely exist. We do not know the meaning of our lives at birth; but we gain knowledge and wisdom from our interactions with people and from our actions and reactions to the situations, we are in. As we discover this meaning, there are certain beliefs and values that we reject and affirm.

Our lives have purpose. This purpose puts all our physical, emotional, and intellectual potentials into use; sustains us during trying times; and gives us something to look forward to—a goal to achieve, a destination to reach. A person without purpose or a life without meaning is like a rudderless ship drifting at sea, at the whim of every wind and wave.

You have to reach in—look inside yourself. Introspection goes beyond recalling the things that happened in a day, week, or month. You need to look closely and reflect on your thoughts, feelings, beliefs, and motivations.

Periodically examining your experiences, the decisions you make, the relationships you have, and the things you engage in, provide useful insights on your life goals, on the good traits you must sustain and the bad traits you have to discard. Moreover, it gives you clues on how to act, react, and conduct yourself in the midst of any situation. Like any skill, introspection can be learned; all it takes is the courage and willingness to seek the truths that lie within you.

Here are some pointers when you introspect:

1. Be objective,

2. be forgiving of yourself, and

3. focus on your areas for improvement.

Develop your true potential

Religion and science have differing views on matters of the human spirit. Religion views people as spiritual beings temporarily living on Earth, while science views the spirit as just one dimension of an individual.

Mastery of the self is a recurring theme in both Christian (Western) and Islamic (Eastern) teachings. The needs of the body are recognized but placed under the needs of the spirit. Beliefs, values, morality, rules, experiences, and good works provide the blueprint to ensure the growth of the spiritual being.

In psychology, realizing one's full potential is to self-actualize. Abraham Maslow (*A Theory of Motivation, 1943*) identified several human needs: physiological, security, belongingness, esteem, cognitive, aesthetic, self-actualization, and self-transcendence. When you have satisfied the basic physiological and emotional needs, spiritual or existential needs come next. Achieving each need leads to the total development of the individual.

Perhaps the difference between these two, religion and psychology, is the respective purpose of self-development: Christianity and Islam see that self-development is a means toward serving God, while psychology views that self-development is an end by itself.

Recognize that we live in a truly interconnected world

Religions stress the concept of our relatedness to all creation, live and inanimate. Thus, we call other people "brothers and sisters" even if there are no direct blood relations. Moreover, deity-centered religions such as Christianity and Islam speak of the relationship between humans and a higher being.

On the other hand, science expounds on our link to other living things through the evolution theory. This relatedness is clearly seen in the concept of ecology, the interaction between living and non-living things.

In psychology, connectedness is a characteristic of self-transcendence, the highest human need according to Maslow. Recognizing your connection to all things makes you more humble and respectful of people, animals, plants, and things in nature. It makes you appreciate everything around you. It moves you to go beyond your comfort zone and reach out to other people, and become stewards of all other things around you. Interconnectivity helps us to grow in spirit as we live through the series of day-to-day encounters. Not all are positive, not all are negative ... the important thing is that we learn from each, and from this knowledge, further spiritual growth is made possible.

Dreams & Goals

Everyone, at some point of his or her life, has dreamed of being somebody special, somebody big somebody fantastically successful.

Many of us have fantasized about being the one who hits the game-winning homer or scores the winning basket or touchdown. Or dreamed of being the homecoming queen, a TV star, actor or successful businessperson. All the things we may aspire to at one time or the other and hold in our hearts. How many times have we dreamed of being rich, or successful, or happy with our relationships?

There is nothing wrong with big dreams and great aspirations. Unfortunately, often the dreams remain just that—dreams instead of experiencing exciting adventures by getting things done to move us towards our goals. Instead of working towards a goal, we are caught up in the humdrum of living from day-to-day and for some that means they just barely exist.

Life could be so much better, if only we learned to not only aim higher (but realistically) and then take action to realize our dreams.

The most common problem to setting goals is the word impossible. Most people get hung up thinking "I can't do this, it's too hard." "It's impossible, no one can do this."

That's a lot of power to give to one word. People turn their whole lives over to that one word. Impossible. If everyone thought that what they dreamed was impossible, there would be no inventions, no innovations, no technology and no breakthroughs in human accomplishment.

Scientists were baffled when they looked at the bumblebee. A very humble insect indeed. Theoretically, they said, it was impossible for the bumblebee to fly. Fortunately, for the bumblebee, no one told to them, so fly it does, *"thank you very much"* say the plants that it pollinates.

Some people suffer from having unrealistic goals and dreams—to make real progress in anything you have to be reasonable—if you are 5 foot tall and weigh 110 pounds, you're probably not going to achieve a dream of playing in the NBA. Some people have reasonable dreams—dreams and goals that they can achieve ... but are not acting on them. The result for both, are broken dreams, and tattered aspirations.

If you load yourself with self-doubt, and self-limiting assumptions, you will never be able to break past what you think is impossible. If you reach too far, without working towards your goal, you will find yourself clinging to that impossible dream. This is a fool's gesture—wasted effort that leads to a wasted life.

Those who just dream without goals and defined steps to take action to achieve them and without working to take those steps, end up disappointed and disillusioned. And frankly, that is what they deserve. You can't just "dream" ... you have to "do". Take action so that your dreams don't rust away or gather dust.

If you told someone a hundred years ago that one day it would be possible to send mail from here to the other side of the world in a few seconds, they would probably say you were out of your mind. But, through people's sheer desire and perseverance, faxes, e-mail and many other impossible dreams are now realities. Imagine where you will be in 20 years if you work each day towards realizing your dreams.

Thomas Edison once said that genius is 1% inspiration and 99% perspiration. Nothing could be truer. For one to accomplish his or her dreams, there has to be had work and discipline. But take note that

that 1% has to be a think-big dream, and not some easily accomplished one. Ask any person who is very physically fit and he or she will tell you that there can be no gains unless you work outside of your comfort zone. Remember the saying, "No pain, no gain"? That is as true as it can be.

Dream on, and don't be caught up with any perceived limitations. Think big and work hard to attain those dreams.

As you step and make the climb towards your dreams, you will find out that the impossible has just become a little bit more possible.

What I write in the next chapter may help you as believing in it and applying it over a long life have helped me.

* * *

Chapter 8 ~ How To Succeed in Life & Reach Any Goal

"Success hinges on getting things done"

The Single Most Important Personal Characteristic Needed for Success (contained in a story called "A Message to Garcia").

Written over 100 years ago (at the time of the Spanish-American War) the following has phrasing that is awkward and stilted compared to today's somewhat relaxed writing styles—but the concept of what it contains is not "out of date" or "out of fashion". In fact, because of the things done wrong, by some people and companies, as of this writing, causing unprecedented damage to the financial markets, our economy and to millions of people—I feel that the "message" contained in "A Message to Garcia" is even more relevant and important today.

Because it was written in "another time" take the reference to "man" or "men" to mean both men and women. It loses none of its import by doing that.

In its day, over 40 million copies were printed and at the time this is said to be a larger circulation than any other literary essay, article or book ever attained during the lifetime of an author, in all history.

Long before I ever read this story, its essence was inside me and to that, I attribute not only much of the successes I've achieved but also the ability to deal with and work through some significant personal and career challenges in my life. "Forging on, through the darkness, into the light on the other side."

People like Rowan (you'll read about him shortly) still exist but more are needed.

A Message to Garcia by Elbert Hubbard (in the public domain):

A Message To Garcia, was written one evening after supper, in a single hour. It was on the 22nd of February, 1899, Washington's Birthday. The thing leaped hot from my heart, written after a trying day, when I had been endeavoring to train some rather delinquent villagers to abjure the comatose state and get radioactive.

The immediate suggestion, though, came from a little argument over the teacups, when my boy Bert suggested that Rowan was the real hero of the Cuban War. Rowan had gone alone and done the thing - carried the message to Garcia.

It came to me like a flash!

Yes, the boy is right, the hero is the man who does his work - who carries the message to Garcia.

I got up from the table, and wrote A Message To Garcia. I thought so little of it that we ran it in the Magazine without a heading. The edition went out, and soon orders began to come for extra copies, a dozen, fifty, a hundred, and when the American News Company ordered a thousand, I asked one of my helpers which article it was that stirred up the cosmic dust.

"It's the stuff about Garcia," he said. The next day a telegram came from George H. Daniels, of the New York Central Railroad thus, "Give price on one hundred thousand Rowan article in pamphlet form - Empire State Express advertisement on back - also how soon can ship."

I replied giving price, and stated we could supply the pamphlets in two years.   Our facilities were small and a hundred thousand booklets looked like an awful undertaking.   The result was that I gave Mr. Daniels permission to reprint the article in his own way.   He issued it in booklet form in editions of half a million.   Two or three of these half-million lots were sent out by Mr. Daniels, and in addition the article was reprinted in over two hundred magazines and newspapers. It has been translated into all written languages.

At the time Mr. Daniels was distributing A Message To Garcia, Prince Hilakoff, Director of Russian Railways, was in this country. He was the guest of the New York Central, and made a tour of the country under the personal direction of Mr. Daniels.

The Prince saw the little book and was interested in it, more because Mr. Daniels was putting it out in big numbers, probably, than otherwise. In any event, when he got home he had the matter translated into Russian, and a copy of the booklet given to every railroad employee in Russia. Other countries then took it up, and from Russia it passed into Germany, France, Spain, Turkey, Hindustan and China.

During the war between Russia and Japan, every Russian soldier who went to the front was given a copy of A Message To Garcia. The Japanese, finding the booklets in possession of the Russian prisoners, concluded it must be a good thing, and accordingly translated it into Japanese.

And on an order of the Mikado, a copy was given to every man in the employ of the Japanese Government, soldier or civilian.

Over forty million copies of A Message To Garcia have been printed.

This is said to be a larger circulation than any other literary venture has ever attained during the lifetime of an author, in all history - thanks to a series of lucky accidents.

Elbert Hubbard-December 1, 1913

A Message to Garcia by Elbert Hubbard

In all this Cuban business there is one man stands out on the horizon of my memory like Mars at perihelion.

When war broke out between Spain and the United States it was very necessary to communicate quickly with the leader of the Insurgents. Garcia was somewhere in the mountain vastness of Cuba - no one knew where.

No mail nor telegraph message could reach him. The President must secure his cooperation, and quickly. What to do! Some one said to the President, "There's a fellow by the name of Rowan will find Garcia for you, if anybody can." Rowan was sent for and given a letter to be delivered to Garcia.

How "the fellow by the name of Rowan" took the letter, sealed it up in an oil-skin pouch, strapped it over

his heart, in four days landed by night off the coast of Cuba from an open boat, disappeared into the jungle, and in three weeks came out on the other side of the Island, having traversed a hostile country on foot, and delivered his letter to Garcia - are things I have no special desire now to tell in detail.

The point that I wish to make is this: President McKinley gave Rowan a letter to be delivered to Garcia; Rowan took the letter and did not ask, "Where is he at?" By the Eternal! There is a man whose form should be cast in deathless bronze and the statue placed in every college of the land. It is not book-learning young men need, nor instruction about this and that, but a stiffening of the vertebrae which will cause them to be loyal to a trust, to act promptly, concentrate their energies: do the thing - "Carry a message to Garcia!" General Garcia is dead now, but there are other Garcia's.

No man who has endeavored to carry out an enterprise where many hands were needed, but has been well nigh appalled at times by the imbecility of the average man - the inability or unwillingness to concentrate on a thing and do it.

Slipshod assistance, foolish inattention, dowdy indifference, and half-hearted work seem the rule and no

man succeeds, unless by hook or crook or threat he forces or bribes other men to assist him; or mayhap, God in His goodness performs a miracle, and sends him an Angel of Light for an assistant. You, reader, put this matter to a test: You are sitting now in your office - six clerks are within call. Summon any one and make this request: "Please look in the encyclopedia and make a brief memorandum for me concerning the life of Correggio."

Will the clerk quietly say, "Yes, sir," and go do the task?

On your life, he will not. He will look at you out of a fishy eye and ask one or more of the following questions:

Who was he?

Which encyclopedia?

Where is the encyclopedia?

Was I hired for that?

Don't you mean Bismarck?

What's the matter with Charlie doing it?

Is he dead?

Is there any hurry?

Sha'n't I bring you the book and let you look it up yourself?

What do you want to know for?

And I will lay you ten to one that after you have answered the questions, and explained how to find the information, and why you want it, the clerk will go off and get one of the other clerks to help him try to find Garcia - and then come back and tell you there is no such man. Of course I may lose my bet, but according to the Law of Average, I will not.

Now, if you are wise, you will not bother to explain to your "assistant" that Correggio is indexed under the C's, not in the K's, but you will smile very sweetly and say, "Never mind," and go look it up yourself. And this incapacity for independent action, this moral stupidity, this infirmity of the will, this unwillingness to cheerfully catch hold and lift -these are the things that put pure Socialism so far into the future. If men will not act for themselves, what will they do when the benefit of their effort is for all?

A first-mate with knotted club seems necessary; and the dread of getting "the bounce" Saturday night holds many a worker to his place. Advertise for a stenographer, and nine out of ten who apply can neither spell nor punctuate – and do not think it necessary to.

Can such a one write a letter to Garcia? "You see that bookkeeper," said the foreman to me in a large factory. "Yes, what about him?" "Well he's a fine accountant, but if I'd send him up town on an errand, he might accomplish the errand all right, and on the other hand, might stop at four saloons on the way, and when he got to Main Street would forget what he had been sent for."

Can such a man be entrusted to carry a message to Garcia?

We have recently been hearing much maudlin sympathy expressed for the "downtrodden denizens of the sweatshop" and the "homeless wanderer searching for honest employment," and with it all often go many hard words for the men in power.

Nothing is said about the employer who grows old before his time in a vain attempt to get frowsy ne'er-do-wells to do intelligent work; and his long, patient striving after "help" that does nothing but loaf when his back is turned.

In every store and factory there is a constant weeding-out process going on. The employer is constantly sending away "help" that have shown their incapacity to further the interests of the business, and others are being taken on.

No matter how good times are, this sorting continues: only, if times are hard and work is scarce, the sorting is done finer - but out and forever out the incompetent and unworthy go.

It is the survival of the fittest. Self-interest prompts every employer to keep the best - those who can carry a

Sky High ~ No Goal Is Out of Your Reach

message to Garcia. I know one man of really brilliant parts who has not the ability to manage a business of his own, and yet who is absolutely worthless to any one else, because he carries with him constantly the insane suspicion that his employer is oppressing, or intending to oppress, him. He cannot give orders; and he will not receive them.

Should a message be given him to take to Garcia, his answer would probably be, "Take it yourself!" Tonight this man walks the streets looking for work, the wind whistling through his threadbare coat. No one who knows him dare employ him, for he is a regular firebrand of discontent.

He is impervious to reason, and the only thing that can impress him is the toe of a thick-soled Number Nine boot. Of course I know that one so morally deformed is no less to be pitied than a physical cripple; but in our pitying, let us drop a tear, too, for the men who are striving to carry on a great enterprise, whose working hours are not limited by the whistle, and whose hair is fast turning white through the struggle to hold in line dowdy indifference, slipshod imbecility, and the heartless ingratitude which, but for their enterprise, would be both hungry and homeless. Have I put the matter too strongly?

Possibly I have; but when all the world has gone a-slumming I wish to speak a word of sympathy for the man who succeeds - the man who, against great odds, has directed the efforts of others, and having succeeded, finds there's nothing in it: nothing but bare board and clothes.

I have carried a dinner pail and worked for day's wages, and I have also been an employer of labor, and I know there is something to be said on both sides. There is no excellence, per se, in poverty; rags are no recommendation; and all employers are not rapacious and high-handed, any more than all poor men are virtuous. My heart goes out to the man who does his work when the "boss" is away, as well as when he is at home. And the man who, when given a letter for Garcia, quietly takes the missive, without asking any idiotic questions, and with no lurking intention of chucking it into the nearest sewer, or of doing aught else but deliver it, never gets "laid off" nor has to go on a strike for higher wages.

Civilization is one long anxious search for just such individuals. Anything such a man asks shall be granted. He is wanted in every city, town and village - in every office, shop, store and factory. The world cries out for such: he is needed and needed badly - the man who can "Carry a Message to Garcia."

I have noticed in my personal and professional life that there are certain people who possess an almost indescribable characteristic—the simple ability to get things done.

You know that type person. It may be an employee, a colleague, or an acquaintance, perhaps even a friend. You ask them to do something and they simply get it done, no questions asked. This is contrasted by the other type of individual who, when assigned a task or asked to get something done, simply never seems to be able to get their arms around it, never seems to comprehend the request, may come back and ask a multitude of meaningless questions, complains, and still never seems to get it right.

Successful people and people who want to be successful in their life, profession or business, get things done and get them done right the majority of the time.

No one's perfect, we all make mistakes but focusing on doing the right things, and how you respond to your mistakes, tells the tale.

Take every opportunity to learn. Continually seek out knew knowledge. Read about and observe the professionals around you. See if what they say or do can have meaning and importance to you. Balance it all against your own common sense.

But in all that you do or undertake, focus on getting things done!

* * *

Getting Unstuck

You or someone you know may have already begun a journey and now feel that the path you've chosen is not the right one for you. Or perhaps, one path has ended and you are ready for a new destination and road to travel.

If you are stuck, or at a point in life and don't know or aren't quite sure what direction to take then I believe the following 7-Steps might help you.

Keep this in mind. For many people money drives them in the choices they make about their life and career. But being passionate about making money can lead you to take on things or get into ventures with only the thought of the money driving your decision.

Is the money important? Absolutely! Is how you make it important? Yes, if making your life more comfortable, certain and suitable for you are some of your goals! This factors in because if you make a wrong choice you could find out that the profession or new path that you've picked became the worst high-pressure and unrewarding situation you ever had.

Here's how to learn from the past and how you personally feel about certain things (what may have lead you to feeling "stuck" or "unsure") and how to use them to find the right path for you:

Step1

Take the elements of the things you have tried in the past that you spent time, effort and perhaps money in learning and/or doing, but that did not work out or just did not feel rewarding to you (and do this for your current position as well if you are currently employed but are seeking to make a change or transition to something else).

Step 2

On a sheet of paper, draw a line down the middle of it. On the left at the top of the page, write "Bad" and on the right top write "Good".

Step 3

For each thing, you have tried and regarding your current job, list out the bad and the good aspects of it; the bad will constitute the determinants of why it did not work out for you or why it did not make you happy or fill you with any passion. The good are the positive elements that helped offset the bad but did not carry enough weight to make it work or rewarding for you.

Step 4

Once you have done that look at what you've written.

Take a new sheet of paper and transfer all the good things to that page. This becomes a profile of the things that were positive that you need to look for in a new profession or opportunity that may present the most attractive and suitable scenario for you.

Step 5

Now with your "Good" profile in front of you, take the profession, market or industry that interests you, think about how you can utilize those good aspects in that profession or opportunity serving that specific market or industry. Make notes about the ones that have those good aspects to them. These should be your focus.

Step 6

Once you've done that calculate what I call your Personal Economic Burden (all your monthly personal expenses that you need to pay to live: mortgage, rent, insurance, food, utilities, car payments, etc.). Total that up and add 30% to it (10% for miscellaneous, 10% for tithing or charitable contributions and at least 10% for your own savings). Take that total amount multiply by 12 and divide by 365. That is the daily amount your new profession or opportunity must generate for you to be "comfortable."

We'll call that the "Comfort Number". That's not making you rich but if you achieve it; it will give you a solid foundation to build on so that you can make even more money if that is your ultimate goal. If you have other sources of income, you can factor that in as well but you want each decision you make about a profession or career to be as self-supporting as possible.

Step 7

When you have that daily number and with it in mind, review your notes from number 5 above and research to determine if you feel that profession or opportunity can generate what you need to meet your Comfort Number. If so, then that is a profession or path you should focus on.

Finally, take time to think things through – never jump blindly or go off on a path that you're not reasonably sure is going to lead you to where you want to go. The above steps will help you.

Self-Management solves many of life's problems: Start taking control

Self-management, goal setting and tracking your results have a lot to do with taking control of your life. They are the ingredients that, used together in the right way, can empower you to do just that.

One aspect of taking control is something that many people don't consider a factor. Having a positive outlook. If you have a negative attitude you're probably not going to care about what is going on around you and don't believe that anything you do can help. Feeling that way makes it a self-fulfilling prophecy.

Being positive has nothing to do with being unrealistically optimistic. It means not letting negative thinking take away the control that you can exert over your life. It allows you to focus on your strengths and accomplishments, which increases happiness and motivation. This, in turn, motivates you to spend more time making progress, and less time feeling down and stuck.

Following are some practical suggestions that you can use to help you shift into a more positive thinking pattern:

Take Good Care of Yourself

It's much easier to be positive when you are eating well, exercising, and getting enough rest.

Remind Yourself of the Things You Are Grateful For

Stress and challenges don't seem quite as bad when you are constantly reminding yourself of the things that are right in life. Taking just 60-seconds a day to stop and appreciate the good things will make a huge difference.

Look for the Proof Instead of Making Assumptions

A fear of rejection leads us to assume that we know what others are thinking, but our fears are usually not reality. Don't waste time worrying about things beyond your control or that you did something wrong unless you have proof that there is something to worry about.

Detach From Negative Thoughts

Your thoughts can't hold any power over you if you don't judge them. If you notice yourself having a negative thought, detach from it, witness it, and don't follow it.

Step On the "ANTs"

In his book *"Change Your Brain, Change Your Life"*, Dr. Daniel Amen talks about "ANTs" - Automatic Negative Thoughts. These are the bad thoughts that are usually reactionary, like "Those people are laughing, they must be talking about me," or "My boss wants to see me? It must be bad!" When you notice these thoughts, realize that they are nothing more than ANTs and squash them!

Interrupt Negative Patterns

If you find yourself stuck or continually thinking of the bad or negative things in your life, a great way to stop it is to interrupt the pattern and force yourself to do something completely different. A hyper-focus on something negative is never productive, because it's not rational or solution-oriented, it's just excessive worry. Try changing your physical environment—go for a walk or sit outside. You could also call a friend, pick up a book, or turn on some music.

Self-management starts with deciding what you really want to do with your personal or professional life (or both) and what short-term and long-term goals you need to reach to achieve it.

Then you have to break down goals into the smaller and manageable targets that you must complete. Once you have your goals defined, waste no time in tackling them!

A good way to break large goals down into manageable pieces is to have a daily and/or weekly set of goals or action to take, tasks to complete, that lead towards accomplishing a larger objective. By doing this you will always have small steps to take that will help you gain traction and progress towards getting things done.

Every day will give you an opportunity to complete a task that gives you a feeling of accomplishment that becomes positive reinforcement and proof that you are in control of your life.

Managing your self is about being focused. The Pareto Principle also known as the '80:20 Rule' states that 80% of efforts that are not managed or are unfocused generate only 20% of the desired output. However, 80% of the desired output can be generated using only 20% of a well-managed effort. That makes sense doesn't it?

Self-management is really a simple set of rules that involves scheduling of appointments, goal setting, thorough planning, creating things to do lists and prioritizing. These are the core basics that should be understood and applied. If they are, they will result in an efficient self-management skill that produces positive results for you.

These basic skills can be refined further to include the finer points of decision-making—an important part of life. Inherent abilities such as emotional intelligence and critical thinking are also essential to your personal growth, which empowers you to take control of your life.

Self-management involves everything you do. No matter how big and no matter how small, everything counts. Each new piece of knowledge you acquire, each new piece of advice you consider, each new skill you develop, should be taken into consideration in the context of your goals and objectives.

Having a balanced life-style should be a main component of managing your life. This is one aspect that many people fail to grasp. Self-management is about getting results, not about being busy.

The six areas any person who feels stuck or that their life is out of control, should seek to improve are physical, intellectual, social, career, emotional and spiritual:

1. The physical aspect involves having a healthy body, which means less stress and fatigue.
2. The intellectual aspect involves education and other activities to expand your learning or understanding.
3. The social aspect involves developing relationships and being an active and responsible contributor to society.
4. The career aspect involves school and work. No getting around that—having the right education background and/or training is essential.
5. The emotional aspect involves your feelings and desires towards your self and others and manifesting them appropriately.
6. The spiritual aspect involves a personal quest for meaning and purpose in your life.

Thoroughly planning and having a set of things to do list for each of the key areas may not be very practical, but determining which area in your life is not given enough attention is key.

Each area creates the whole you, if you are ignoring one area then you ignore an important part of yourself.

Self-management should not be a daunting task. It is a very sensible and reasonable approach in solving problems big or small. A great way to begin to lay the groundwork is to follow several basic activities.

Review your goals often whether they are immediate or long-term objectives. A way to do this is to keep a list that is always accessible to you. Always determine what task is necessary or not necessary to achieve your goals. And which activities help you maintain a balanced life style.

Each of us has a peak time and a time when we slow down, these are our natural cycles. We should be able to tell when to do the difficult tasks and do them when we are the sharpest.

Other important items are:

- Learning to say "No". You actually see this advice often. Heed it even if it involves saying the word to family or friends. You can't always "do everything for everyone."
- Try to get the cooperation from people around you who actually benefit from your efforts at self-management.
- Don't procrastinate. Attend to necessary things immediately.
- Have a positive attitude and set yourself up for success. But be realistic in your approach in achieving your goals.

Self-management is the art and science of building a better life.

From the moment, you integrate it into your life; you open up a broad spectrum of solutions to help get things moving in the right direction for you. It also creates more doors for opportunities to knock on. The benefits of setting goals as part of self-management is no secret to top-caliber athletes (who use their goals as a target for their training for self-improvement), successful businessmen and businesswomen and all types of achievers in all different fields of professional and personal development.

Goal setting gives you short-term and long-term motivation and focus. They help you focus on the acquisition of required knowledge and help you to plan and organize your resources and your time so that you can get the best out of your life.

Setting clearly defined short term and long-term goals will enable you to measure your progress and achieve personal satisfaction once you have successfully met your goals.

Tracking your progress will also enable you to see the stages of completion leading to the actual realization of your goals. This eliminates the feeling of a long and pointless grind towards achieving your goal.

Your self-confidence and level of competence will also improve, as you will be more aware of your capabilities as you complete or achieve your goals.

Here are some points that should be taken into consideration in setting goals and achieving them:

1. Attitude plays a very big role in setting and achieving your goals. You must ask yourself if any part of you or your mind is holding you back towards completing your simplest objectives.

2. If there is any part of your behavior that is slowing you down or preventing you from meeting your goals (both small and large) or disrupts your plans; then the immediate thing to do is to address this problem and resolve it. Don't let it dictate what you can accomplish in life.

3. Successful Careers (and lives) are made by good (reasonable) goal setting and then doing the work to accomplish them. Failing in a

career is often attributed to simply not having a plan, of if having one, not getting things done to execute your plan. Careers require a lot from an individual, which often makes the "career" the life of the individual. Plan how far you want to go into your career so that you know the steps you need to take to get there. Caution: remember that a strong successful life (in all areas) requires balance.

4. Education and/or training are key in achieving your goals. If your goals require you to have a certain kind of degree or require a certain specialization or demand a certain skill to be developed, make plans to get the appropriate education.

5. Your family should never be left out of your plans. If you are just starting a family then you have to decide if you want to be a parent or when you want to become a parent. You also have to know if you really would be a good parent and how well would you relate to extended family members.

6. Personal financial situations also play a major role in achieving your goals. Have a realistic goal on how much you are able to earn. If you want to make more money, you also must be able to create plans or set stages to work towards by which you will be able to increase your earning potential.

7. As the saying goes, "All work and no play makes Jack a dull boy," or something to that effect. It is by all means true down to the last the letter. Rewarding yourself should be included into your plans.

To start achieving your lifetime goals, set a quarter of a century plan, then break it down to 5 year plans then break it down again to 1 year plans, then 6 month plans then monthly plans, then weekly, then daily. Then create a things-to-do list for the day. Always review your plans and prepare for contingencies.

Goal setting is not the easiest thing to do, if they are meaningful to you and you are serious about accomplishing them. But they are a necessary part managing and taking control of your life.

* * *

In her book, *"Playing by the Unwritten Rules – Moving from the middle to the top"*, the Author, Indigo Triplett Johnson makes the following observations that I agree with:

> *"People spend an inordinate amount of time searching for the ideal job versus managing their career," page-59.*

"In determining your passion, you must recognize where you are now, and with candor, address whether this is where you want to be, and more importantly, recognize how you got here," page-62.

"In determining your passion, you should think of yourself as a compilation of all your knowledge, skills, abilities, and personal characteristics," page-61.

* * *

"If you can look into the seeds of time and say which grain will grow and which will not, speak then to me."

- The Bard, Macbeth

I don't know anyone who can foretell the future. Do you?

That is why it is common sense to do the things that you should, to prepare yourself for what happens in

160 |

life. Life is not a passive activity. You have to participate. You have to engage life and take some measure of control. Being able to manifest control means you have to have that ability or create it if that is something you lack. You should do the following:

- Continue to educate yourself, broadening your knowledge base.

- Take care of your health.

- Work on your personal and professional relations so that you handle and develop them in the best possible ways.

- Have respect for your self—if you don't no one else will.

"The reasonable man adapts himself to the world. The unreasonable man persists in trying to adapt the world to himself. Therefore, all progress depends on the unreasonable man."

- George Bernard Shaw

The above should be considered a "universal truth". The world is populated in the majority by those who adapt and "give way" to the world. It shapes them and they feel they have little to do that can affect that.

The "movers" of the world view things differently. The world does have impact on them but they shape the outcome of their efforts. They don't accept only what the world gives them; they reach out and grab what they want by adapting their world to create opportunities for themselves.

Sometimes you have to be "unreasonable" in order to move ahead and get the things that you want from life. Never be afraid to be a non-conformist if doing that is what you need to do to achieve your goals.

Never hesitate to believe that there is good in the world and that the bad is just something that comes with life and you have to deal with it when it appears.

I believe that life gives us tremendous opportunities. I also know that it gives us challenges that can sometimes seem insurmountable. The thing of it is that success in life (or so I believe) is all in how you react to what happens to you. As Rudyard Kipling put it in his poem "If":

If you can meet with Triumph and Disaster,

And treat those two impostors just the same;

By that, I believe he means deal with things evenly, in proportion, take the "bad" with the "good", and understand that you will encounter both in life.

The Navy has a phrase that I'll borrow. "Take an even strain." Originally it was intended for sailors who were handling lines (the ropes used to moor ships to a pier or that were used when handling a transfer of some object or person between two ships underway) so that they would not pull too hard or slack off too much (both could result in an accident or injury). It also came to have a similar meaning, at least to many with military backgrounds, to not over or under react.

Success in life requires we come up with the right response more times than not. The right level of response is something that we all have to figure out as appropriate for us in the context of our situation.

With that in mind, and knowing that life deals out good and bad to all of us. I try to take an "even strain" in all matters. You should too.

And as Kipling put near the closing of "If", if you can deal well with most things that go on in life:

"Then Yours is the Earth and all that is in it."

I believe that it is in the "managing" of where you are that gets you to where you want to go.

If you are stuck in a job or career that you do not like or love, then manage circumstance—bend them—and work towards change. The years of your life will roll on—take an active hand in guiding how they unfold.

The Eternal Years

We peep within the opening door,

And in this strange new House of Life

We gaze around.

A sunbeam's flash, a shadow's pall

Light on us — and we rise or fall,

While Thine eternal years roll on.

A month to most — a year to few,

A sheaf of years mayhap to some,

But ere our lips have learned Earth's speech,

Before our hands her fruit can reach

The signals flash. Pass on.

We know not what Thou would'st with us,

Whither we go or whence we came.

Down through the darkness of the night

We move, and back again to light.

While Thine eternal years roll on.

A grain of dust by winds hurled forth

We spin along life's untried road —

Whirl in its eddy for a space,

And then return — each to his place.

While Thine eternal years roll on.

Each to his place. Ah, be it so,

Not purposeless our little span.

Where we see chaos order reigns

On those illimitable plains

Where Thine eternal years roll on.

We know not what Thou would'st with us,

Whither we go or whence we came.

Down through the darkness of the night

We move, and back again to light

While Thine eternal years roll on.

Chapter Nine ~ In Closing

I am very proud of my accomplishments and attribute my success to having dedicated mentors and having the determination to get things done.

Even though I was an honor student and enjoyed studying, I never dreamed of earning silver flight nurse wings, earning a doctorate, becoming a Major General in the United States Air Force and Air National Guard and a White House political appointee. But of all those levels of accomplishment, my greatest joy in life is mentoring and helping others to achieve their goals and become successful. As my mentors have helped me.

I cannot think of anyone who was born "all-knowing" or "all-seeing". By that I mean life is a never-ending series of learning events—experiences and interactions with others that fill up the vessel of our mind. Our first and often most important forms of education are the example and direction we receive from our parents. They are truly our life's first mentors.

Those mentors are supplemented and added to by church and school—an additional source distinctly different from the mentoring we receive from parents but that becomes just as beneficial and in some ways even more powerful in providing a sense of self-empowerment. Theirs is a belief in us that does not come from the ties of family or blood—they believe in us based on an independent assessment of potential.

No matter their source, a mentor brings to us the perspective of experience-based knowledge that can help us and very often cuts down on the learning curve and accelerates our progress.

A mentor is a counselor, coach, motivator, champion, and role model. A mentor is a person who has a sincere desire to enhance the success of others. Mentors generally play various roles at different stages in life and for many successful people—mentors have made all the difference in their worlds.

Given that mentoring plays such an important role in our development it seems it would fall into the other categories of significant things that we protect (or plan for) by having insurance. Most of us, in our lives, have medical insurance from birth to death and certainly have life insurance at some point. We have car insurance, and are able to buy other types of coverage such as pet and vacation insurance. Yet we do not have insurance to ensure the continuum of training and education as we move through life. Mentoring insurance.

But perhaps "insurance" is not the right word maybe what we need is more along the lines of mentoring "assurance." The assurance that comes with belief in yourself, strengthened when others believe in you too.

We can invest in real estate, a whole host of commodities such as gold and oil, even in the currencies of major nations and of course the stock markets—but how can you invest in mentoring?

Here's how you do it:

Whether you are young or old, if you are starting out in a new direction, taking a new path or breathing fresh life into your existence—chances are that there is someone who has "been there, done that" and can guide you and/or even help you along the way. Invest in the effort to find that type of person. Reach out to them and ask for help. That is how you, the person who can use some direction makes an investment—in your self.

If you are an older or experienced person, be willing to respond to those who seek you and ask for help. When you mentor, you invest in the human potential stock market and build bridges for others to pass over to reach success. These investments provide benefits and rewards, today, tomorrow and for a lifetime.

"The basis of a true mentoring relationship should be a rewarding experience for the mentor and protégé"

- Indigo Triplett Johnson, "Playing by the Unwritten Rules--Moving from the middle to the top" (2006 page 47).

Our success in the future depends on how well we nurture, educate, manage, and instill social consciousness and responsibility in our young people. The success of our nations military, government and corporate America depends on how well we educate and mentor our youth. Mentoring is perhaps the best tool for ensuring social viability as it is proven to develop people that are better prepared for the challenges that everyone faces in life.

"Look for qualities in a mentor that you would admire in a life partner: integrity, good communicator, open-minded, informative, a good listener, dependable, knowledgeable, resourceful, results-oriented, flexible, attentive, and so forth."

- Indigo Triplett Johnson, "Playing by the Unwritten Rules--Moving from the middle to the top" (2006 page 49).

As we step deeper into the 21st century, we can rest assured the challenges of competition in a fast-paced, technology-driven, internationally aligned political and economic environment will demand that those aiming for positions of top leadership are the best educated and prepared for those roles.

New waves of bright, eager workers are at the door, waiting to get in and propel themselves to the heights of professional achievement. These achievements contribute significantly toward improving the quality of life and benefit our society at all levels. Thus improving the educational and economic status of our citizens, ultimately results in positive results for our country and the world at large.

Remember this...

Our deepest fear is not that we are inadequate.
Our deepest fear is that we are powerful beyond measure.

It is our light not our darkness that most frightens us.

We ask ourselves, who are we to be brilliant, gorgeous, talented and fabulous.

Actually, who are we not to be...You playing small doesn't serve the world.

There is nothing enlightened about shrinking so other people won't feel insecure around you...

And as we let our light shine, we unconsciously give other people permission to do the same.

As we are liberated from our own fear, our presence automatically liberates others!

- Nelson Mandela

In spite of numerous roadblocks in my life, my goal was to turn obstacles into steppingstones and move up the career ladder so I could manifest my own form of leadership to directly and positively affect those who worked for me and those I worked with.

This was for my family, my community, my state and my country.

Few people today understand the difficulties faced and personal sacrifices required of minorities and women of past eras who elected to serve their country in the military. For them the journey continues, even though laws and policies are in place on equal opportunity. While we have made monumental advances, there is no time to rest on our laurels.

We still have a lot of work to do. Minorities and women are moving up and are continuing to serve with honor and distinction around this great nation. Like others, they should be recognized for their contributions. Not because they are minority or female; because they are highly skilled and competent officers, enlisted and civilian professionals. Because they chose to serve their country then and now.

I do not forget that I am here today and have accomplished the things I have because the pioneers, that went before me charted the course. They made it possible for me and others to serve in significant military and civilian roles. I simply followed their path—extending it just a little. Young people out there today and tomorrow will extend this path to immeasurable distances because they are destined for even higher roles and greatness!

By working together as a team, we can build bridges for others to pass over and to add value to America—because we have promises to keep for our veterans, our family, our community, our state and our country.

Remember these simple points to help you along the way:

- Embrace a persistent commitment to hard work and always strive for excellence. Just getting by is not acceptable.

- Take advantage of every opportunity to learn and to improve yourself.

- Prepare yourself by seeking advanced education, challenging projects and visualizing the future, and

- Seek mentoring from various outstanding leaders, civilian and military.

With this—remember that the future is the bright light ahead of you. Walk toward that light, and enjoy your journey:

- Never evade the challenges—face them squarely. That should be your motto.

- Reach out for opportunities. That should be your goal.

- Accept your responsibilities. That must be your mission.

- With preparation, hard work, education, mentoring and God's help, nothing can stop you.

We have some grave challenges facing us as a nation. Do we have the intelligence, humor, imagination, courage, tolerance, love, respect, and will to meet these challenges?

I say yes, because, it is the human spirit that will propel us to success:

- Money cannot buy it,

- Power cannot compel it,

- Technology cannot create it,

Our success can only come from the human spirit!

To young people reading this you have a responsibility to focus on your God given talents and to do your very best in school.

You must:

- Sit at the front of the room,

- Listen to the message,

- Take notes, and

- Boldly step up to the leadership challenge of service to your family, community, state and nation.

- Succeed, because our families, state and our country depends on you.

I hope my experiences and accomplishments will inspire and propel you to immeasurable heights in your personal and professional endeavors. Joseph Conrad said: *"And now the old ships and their men are gone; the new ships and the new men have taken up their watch on the stern-and-impatient sea which offers no opportunities but to those who know how to grasp them with a ready hand and an undaunted heart."* I hope that you see life as a world of opportunities, that you pursue them with that undaunted heart, and grasp them with ready hands, to make them your own.

Yours truly,

Dr. Irene Trowell-Harris

Arlington, Virginia - December 2009

Over the Course of A Life

I've included this for the young members of my family ... and hopefully for young people of all families ... to read and understand that no matter your background or circumstances—you can achieve anything in life that you set as a goal and work towards.

Only two generations away from slavery—without financial resources—in a time when being black and a woman put you at a disadvantage and limited the choices life had to offer—I carved out success. You can too!

Bio: Dr. Irene Trowell-Harris

Extensive senior executive management and leadership experience in the health care industry, including the civilian, military and federal sectors. Knowledge of the legislative process and health care delivery systems. Experience with Joint Commission on Accreditation of Healthcare Organizations and other regulatory agencies. Performed national oversight of quality assurance/quality improvement including women's health programs, policies, and legislation. Prepared, reviewed, and presented Congressional testimony.

EXPERIENCE

Director, Center for Women Veterans, Office of the Secretary, *October 2001 to present,* Department of Veterans Affairs (VA), Washington, DC

Monitors and coordinates programs, policies, and legislation for America's 1.8 million women veterans. Serves as the primary advisor to the Secretary of Veterans Affairs on programs and all issues related to women veterans.

Director, Northeast Region, Office of Healthcare Inspections, *August 2000 to September 2001.* Department of Veterans Affairs, Office of Inspector General (54C), Washington, DC.

Directed a multidisciplinary staff of inspectors responsible for conducting oversight reviews to improve the economy, effectiveness, and efficiency of VA programs nationally.

Conducted Congressionally mandated Combined Assessment Program (CAP) reviews to evaluate how well medical centers were accomplishing their mission of providing quality patient care and improving access to care, with high patient satisfaction. Inspected and completed Hotline, Oversight, Technical, and Congressional reviews.

Director, Patient Care Inspections and Program Evaluation, *August 1993 to July 2000.*

Managed a nation-wide program on Quality Assurance/Quality Improvement, clinical inspections, and oversight of 163 hospitals, 820 ambulatory care and community-based clinics, 140 nursing homes and 40 domiciliaries.

Assistant to the Director, Air National Guard (ANG) for Human Resources Readiness, Major General, (Active Reserve), Crystal City, VA, *September 1998 to September 2001*

Responsible for readiness, mentoring, women and diversity issues, and related human resources concerns.

ANG Assistant to the Director for Medical Readiness and Nursing Services; Brigadier General, Corporate Headquarters United States Air Force, Office of the Surgeon General, Bolling AFB, Washington, DC, *February 1993 to August 1998*

ANG Policy Advisor/Health Program, *July 1987 to February 1993*

Active duty, Colonel, Corporate Headquarters United States Air Force, Office of the Surgeon General, Bolling AFB, Washington, DC.

Coordinated headquarters-level health policy, program development, congressional hearings and information systems issues with senior representatives in DoD, regulatory agencies, federal and civilian executive organizations.

Senior Staff Specialist for Social and Economic Policy, *August 1985 to July 1987*

American Nurses Association, Corporate Headquarters, Kansas City and Washington, DC.

Collected data for policy formulation on health practice, education, research, economics, and program development for 54 constituent states and the nation's 2 million nurses.

Nurse Consultant and Coordinator, *January 1974 to July 1985*

Departments of Nursing and Psychiatry, Our Lady of Mercy Medical Center, Bronx, NY.

Analyzed and evaluated policy and practice issues based on regulatory agency standards and guidelines.

Positions from 1959-1973 not included—this bio and CV has been shortened to accommodate the planned size of this book.

EDUCATION

- Doctorate (EdD) and Master of Education (EdM) in Health Education, Columbia University, NY, 1983.
- Master of Public Health (MPH) in Public Health Administration, Yale University, New Haven, CT, 1973.
- Bachelor of Arts (BA) in Health Education, Jersey City State College, Jersey City, NJ, 1971, Cum Laude.
- Diploma in Nursing, Registered Nurse (RN), Columbia Hospital School of Nursing, Columbia, SC, 1959.

PROFESSIONAL MEMBERSHIPS

- Senior Executive Association
- Sigma Theta Tau
- Kappa Delta Pi Honor Society
- American Nurses Association
- Advisory Council, Business and Professional Women/USA
- New York State Nurses Association
- National Advisory Council, Alliance of National Defense
- Virginia State Nurses Association
- American Public Health Association
- Association of Military Surgeons of the United States
- Ex officio member of the Defense Advisory Committee on Women in the Services (DACOWITS)
- Women in Military Service for America

RECOGNITION AND AWARDS

- Numerous awards and recognition from the Department of Veteran Affairs
- Commendation from Mike Honda, Member of Congress for service to country and serving as Grand Marshal for Veterans Day Parade, San Jose, CA, November 2007.
- Selected as Distinguished Alumni of Yale University for 2006
- Selected by Women's eNews as one of "21 Leaders for the 21st Century for 2006" in the category of "Seven Who Construct New Realities." 2006
- Honored October 2006 by the Dr. Mae Jemison Foundation of Excellence for contributions to aviation and mentoring.
- Combined Federal Campaign Recognition 2006
- Selected as Distinguished Alumni of Columbia University for 2005
- Certificate of Appreciation VA's 75th Anniversary Celebration 2005

- Dr. James Weaver Society Award 2002
- VA Federal Women's Program Mentoring Recognition
- Special Congressional Recognition Award 1997
- Numerous Military Decorations and Citations
- Senior Flight Nurse Wings
- Received a political appointment at the Department of Veterans Affairs from the White House October 2001

Honored by the Department of Epidemiology and Public Health (EPH), Yale University School of Medicine as Distinguished Alumni 2006, selected on June 1, 2001, for outstanding dedication to public service, and inducted into the EPH Public Service Honor Roll.

Inducted into the Columbia University Nursing Hall of Fame October 1999. Honored by Teachers College, Columbia University, March 4, 1995, as a distinguished alumna and nurse for 1995.

Honorary Degree, Doctor of Humane Letters from the Medical University of South Carolina, May 16, 1997, for outstanding achievements in the field of nursing, the military and the community.

Community Mentoring Award and Tuskegee Airmen, Inc., Chapter named in my honor, at the 105th Airlift Wing, Newburgh, NY, 1999.

Retired from the United States Air Force/Air National Guard on September 30, 2001. Served for 38 years, attained the rank of Major General (two stars), and was awarded the Air Force Distinguished Service, Legion of Merit and New York State Conspicuous Service medals.

Presented numerous keynote speeches nationally and internationally on legislation, leadership, team building, mentoring, educational opportunities, health care issues, women's benefits and services to various organizations including Congress, university, political, federal, state, private; youth, women's and minority groups.

Air Force representative to the Committee on Women
in the NATO Forces Conference held in Istanbul,
Turkey.

Life Highlights

- Presented the keynote address for
  commencement at Embry-Riddle Aeronautical
  University on May 6, 2006. Recognized with
  the Eagle of Aviation Award for significant and
  notable contributions to aviation. The
  ceremony included over 3,500 students,
  parents, friends, veterans, media, dignitaries,
  faculty members, and Reserve Officer Training
  Corps (ROTC) students from the Air Force,
  Army, and Naval ROTC programs. Embry-
  Riddle Aeronautical University, is considered
  the "world's leader in aviation and aerospace
  higher education" and has educated and
  inspired a nation of professionals to become
  aviators, engineers, computer scientists,
  meteorologists, and air traffic managers. The

speech included congratulatory and inspirational remarks, and expressed support for the President's Management Agenda and the Global War on Terrorism. Advised graduating students to not necessarily follow where the path may lead, but to boldly go where there is no path and leave a trail for those who come behind.

- Selected by Women's eNews as one of 21 Leaders for the 21st Century for 2006 in the category of "Seven Who Construct New Realities." Selected from hundreds of nominations representing the United States and overseas. This included women in law, academia, economics, labor, science, business, women's advocacy, engineering, policy and journalism. Honored in NYC May 16, 2006. This award was given for being a national advocate for women veterans.

- Recipient of Yale University's 2006 Distinguished Alumni Award (from Yale University's Department of Epidemiology and

Public Health, School of Medicine) and was honored June 2, 2006 at Yale in New Haven, CT for outstanding contributions to leadership, community activities, women veteran advocacy, public health practice, and support for research and scholarships. Unanimously selected for this award, which recognizes an alumnus who exemplifies the highest level of achievement in leadership, service to Yale, and service to the public.

- Member of the Business and Professional Women/USA Advisory Council (July 05) for initiative "Women Joining Forces - Closing Ranks, Opening Doors" designed to support women veterans. "Founded through a grant from the United States War Council in 1919, BPW/USA is proud to launch this initiative in continuation of the legacy of mobilizing workingwomen during times of crisis," said BPW/USA President Ridgeway. "This initiative reinforces BPW membership's ongoing support of military women and their families."

- Nominated and selected for the Third Annual 2002 James D. Weaver Society Award. The award was named in honor of Dr. Weaver a distinguished former Congressman and Air National Guard Flight Surgeon. The ward was presented at the 102 Annual AMSUS Conference in Louisville, KY on November 11, 2003 at the Society reception. This award is given to a military officer or enlisted member for exemplary military service of any branch (Army or Air) who personifies Integrity First, Service Before Self and Excellence in All They do.

- Retired from the United States Air Force/Air National Guard on 30 September 2001. Served over 38 years, attained the rank of Major General, and was awarded the Air Force Distinguished Service and New York State Conspicuous Service medals. In addition, was awarded the Legion of Merit.

- Honored by the Department of Epidemiology and Public Health (EPH), Yale University

School of Medicine, June 1, 2001 for
outstanding dedication to public service and
inducted into the EPH Public Service Honor
Roll.

- Honored on March 22, 2001 as one of the "25
Influential Black Women in Business" by The
Network Journal (TNJ) at the New York Hilton
and Towers Hotel. Individuals are selected
based on having achieved significant levels of
success in their business and professional
careers.

- Honored by the 369th
Historical Society at the
7th Regiment Armory in
New York City for
extraordinary
accomplishments
achieved in the military
over 38 years of
honorable service,
March 18, 2001.

- Inducted (charter member) into the Teachers College, Columbia University Nursing Hall of Fame, 8 October 1999, New York, New York. As a distinguished alumnus of Columbia University.

- In February 1999, became the first person in National Guard history to have a Mentoring Award named in her honor. The Major General Irene Trowell-Harris Mentoring Award, 105th Airlift Wing, Newburgh, New York.

- On the American Association of University Women Greater Columbia Chapter 1999 Calendar. Also the Women In Military Services Foundation Memorial Calendar for 1999.

- In August 1998, became the first female in history to have a Tuskegee Airmen, Inc. Chapter named in her honor. The Major General Irene Trowell-Harris Chapter, Tuskegee Airmen, Inc., Stewart Air National Guard Base, Newburgh, New York.

- Honored by the Department of Defense and the National Guard as the first African-American female in the 359-year history of the Guard to be promoted to general officer (October 29, 1993). Promoted to Major General September 1, 1998. The highest-ranking African American female in the National Guard.

- Received special congressional recognition on September 12, 1997 by the United States Congress, Black Caucus for outstanding and invaluable service to the community, Washington, DC.

- Awarded an Honorary Degree Doctor of Humane Letters by the Medical  University of South Carolina May 16, 1997 for outstanding achievements in the field of nursing, the military and the community.

- Air Force representative 1997 for the Committee on Women in the North Atlantic Treaty Organization (NATO) Conference, Istanbul, Turkey.

- Ex-Officio for VA, Defense Advisory Committee on Women in the Services (DACOWITS)

- Air Force speaker representing the United States at the 1996 International Conference on Women in Defense, Johannesburg, South Africa.

- Honored by Teachers College, Columbia University, March 4, 1995 as a distinguished alumni and nurse for 1995.

- Attended formal inaugural balls and events in Washington, DC for President George H. W. Bush, President William J. Clinton, President George W. Bush and President Barrack H. Obama.

To Irene Trowell-Harris
With respect and appreciation,

LaVergne, TN USA
11 June 2010
185835LV00003B/2/P